Sovieticus

Sovieticus

American Perceptions and
Soviet Realities

EXPANDED TO COVER THE GORBACHEV PERIOD

STEPHEN F. COHEN

W · W · NORTON & COMPANY

NEW YORK · LONDON

FIRST EDITION

The text of this book is composed in photocomposition Times Roman, with display type set in Typositor Latin Bold and Janson. Composition by the Haddon Craftsmen. Book design by Marjorie J. Flock.

First published as a Norton paperback 1986

Library of Congress Cataloging in Publication Data
Cohen, Stephen F.
  Sovieticus: American perceptions and Soviet realities.

  Includes index.
  1. United States—Foreign relations—Soviet Union—Addresses, essays, lectures. 2. Soviet Union—Foreign relations—United States—Addresses, essays, lectures. 3. Soviet Union—Politics and government—1975– —Addresses, essays, lectures. I. Title.
E183.8.S65C64 1985   327.73047   85–2949

ISBN 0-393-30338-1

W. W. Norton & Company, Inc.,
500 Fifth Avenue, New York, N. Y. 10110
W. W. Norton & Company Ltd.,
37 Great Russell Street, London WC1B 3NU

4 5 6 7 8 9 0

Contents

Introduction: "Sovieticus"

THIS SMALL BOOK FOR general readers is the result of an experiment in scholarly journalism. In 1982, as a professor who had written about the Soviet Union primarily for other specialists and for university students, I began a monthly column called "Sovieticus" in *The Nation* magazine. The purpose was to apply my scholarly and firsthand knowledge of the Soviet Union to current events, and to do so in a style accessible to nonspecialists. All except three of the pieces I have written since October 1982 are reprinted here.

So far as I know, no other column devoted to Soviet affairs now exists in the English-language press, or possibly anywhere outside the Communist world. Indeed, for better or worse, "Sovieticus" may be the first such attempt at scholarly journalism. In the past, a few British and American newspapermen, who had become specialists, wrote regular commentary on Soviet affairs.[1] Unfortu-

---

1. Among them were Edward Crankshaw in *The Observer* of London, Paul Wohl in the *Christian Science Monitor* and Victor Zorza in the *Manchester Guardian*

nately, that tradition has died out. Several journalists have also written scholarly books about the Soviet Union.[2] But until now, it seems, no academic Sovietologist has tried to adapt scholarly perspectives to journalism by writing on a regular schedule in a designated—and, by academic custom, limited—space.

I decided to try partly out of an ambivalence toward journalism. On the one hand, I admired the profession, particularly the work of its best foreign reporters. Indeed, in the late 1970s, I came close to leaving the university in order to become Moscow correspondent for an American newspaper. On the other hand, as a professor, I was often dismayed by the news media's commentary on my area of study, especially as the American-Soviet détente of the 1970s gave way to a new period of cold war.

The problem, as I see it, is that too much American newspaper and television coverage is one-dimensional, speculative or otherwise misleading. Consider, for example, the media image of the Soviet Union that has prevailed in recent years: a crisis-ridden and decaying system that includes a stagnant and unworkable economy; a "sick" society and cynical populace; a corrupt bureaucratic elite; and an alternately reckless and paralyzed leadership. There are elements of truth in that picture, but on the whole it is a caricature, lacking context, complexity and balance. It is akin to those Soviet depictions of American life based largely on accounts of unemployment, drug addiction, street crime and political corruption.

---

and *Washington Post.* A handful of Russian émigrés also wrote regularly on Soviet affairs, notably Boris I. Nicolaevsky in *The New Leader.*

2. They include the Americans William Henry Chamberlin, Louis Fischer and Harrison E. Salisbury.

Why is press coverage of the Soviet Union so inadequate? In the following pages, I suggest some partial answers, including official Soviet secretiveness and censorship, the lack of a fulltime American press corps of specialists in Soviet affairs and the media's tendency to assume the worst about the Soviet Union. The problem is not a new one, nor is it explained simply by the kind of anti-Sovietism that informs much press commentary today. Since the Russian Revolution, both pro-Soviet and anti-Soviet biases have periodically distorted American news accounts, sometimes in the same newspaper.[3] Misreporting the Soviet Union may even be an unalterable tradition. As Will Rogers observed many years ago, "Russia is a country that no matter what you say about it, it's true."[4]

To be fair, there are important exceptions in the press, and journalists themselves are increasingly critical of the profession's coverage of Soviet affairs.[5] But even the critics too often evade the issue by pleading a lack of reliable knowledge. Confronted with failed predictions or baffling

---

3. It may be unfair to single out the *New York Times,* whose recent Moscow correspondents have been among the best, but it is a pertinent example. During the revolution and civil war of 1917–21, the newspaper featured anti-Soviet reports assuring readers that the evil Communist government had fallen or soon would. In the 1930s, dispatches of its pro-Soviet correspondent, Walter Duranty, often read like little more than a Stalinist cover-up. For these episodes in American journalism, see Walter Lippmann and Charles Merz, "A Test of the News," supplement to *The New Republic,* August 4, 1920; Phillip Knightley, *The First Casualty* (New York, 1975), Chapter 7; and James William Crowl, *Angels in Stalin's Paradise* (Washington, 1982).

4. A newspaperman recently brought this quote to the attention of readers (Leonard Silk, the *New York Times,* January 4, 1984).

5. One example is *Inside Story*'s two-part analysis of American coverage, shown on PBS television on April 7 and 14, 1983. Similarly, see Harrison E. Salisbury, "What's Missing from TV's Reports on the Soviets," *TV Guide,* July 10, 1982, pp. 2–6.

evidence, for example, reporters never tire of quoting Winston Churchill's misconceived aphorism that Russia is "a riddle wrapped in a mystery inside an enigma."

That excuse, which puts the Soviet Union in some perverse realm forever beyond our understanding, is no longer valid, if indeed it ever was. Although much remains unknown, Western scholars have learned and published a great deal about the Soviet system. Given the importance the American media attach to the subject, there is no good reason why journalists have not become more familiar with the scholarly literature.

The "Sovieticus" column has been my small attempt to narrow the distance between scholarship and journalism. As a citizen, I have felt the need to comment on the state of American-Soviet relations from my own perspective that détente is both imperative and possible. But my overriding purpose has been analytical: to relate current Soviet events to underlying trends and larger themes; to provide the necessary historical and political context; to replace gray stereotypes with multicolored realities; and thus to help readers achieve a better understanding.

I cannot judge the extent to which I have succeeded or failed. In starting the column in *The Nation,* I hoped that at least a few daily newspapers would also print it, giving me some regular syndication and a wider readership. In that respect, the column has been modestly successful.

Letters from readers have been my only other indication of its reception. Not surprisingly, given the political controversy stirred in the United States by Soviet affairs, the letters have varied greatly. In addition to readers approving of what I wrote or raising thoughtful questions, some have denounced me as an anti-Soviet "demonologist" and urged *The Nation* to get rid of me. Many others, sometimes offering similar advice to the newspapers that carried my column or to my university, have accused me of being a "Soviet apologist."

Critics on both sides may look for support in the official Soviet reaction. Several of the columns disapproving of American policy or the media have been favorably quoted in the Soviet press, and heavily censored versions of at least two of them were even reprinted. And yet, for the past three years, for reasons that may or may not have been related to the column, Soviet authorities denied me permission to visit the country.

For this book, I decided to arrange the columns in topical rather than chronological order. Where appropriate, I have converted them from the present tense, in which they were written, to the past tense. Otherwise, apart from some minor updating to take into account events through the emergence of Mikhail Gorbachev as the new Soviet leader, they appear as they did in *The Nation.* The date at the end of each piece is the cover date of the issue in which that column appeared. Usually, it was written two weeks earlier.

Despite the burdens inflicted on my life by deadlines, I am grateful to Victor S. Navasky, *The Nation*'s editor, for giving me monthly space for roughly 950 words and the complete freedom to write as I saw fit. I am also indebted to two other editors of the magazine, Richard Lingeman and JoAnn Wypijewski, for their vigilant attention to matters of clarity and style. Finally, I must acknowledge the work of other scholars in the field, including those who do not share my perspectives on the Soviet Union and those who disapprove of mixing scholarship and journalism.

S.F.C.

New York City
March 1985

Introduction to the Paperback Edition

I HAVE CONSIDERABLY EXPANDED the paperback edition by adding nine columns written since the hardcover went to press in 1985. They carry my analysis of Soviet affairs and U.S.-Soviet relations beyond Gorbachev's first year in power. For the opportunity to make these additions, and for much else, I am indebted to James Mairs, my friend and editor at W. W. Norton. I should update one other matter. After having been denied a visa for three years, in 1985 I was able to make two trips to the Soviet Union. Some of what I learned during those visits is reflected in the new columns included here.

S.F.C.

New York City
June 1986

I

American Perceptions and Soviet Realities

Sovietophobia: Our Other
Soviet Problem

THE UNITED STATES has two Soviet problems. One is the real but manageable Soviet threat to our national security and international interests.

The second, and increasingly more serious, problem is Sovietophobia, or exaggerated fear of that Soviet threat. An old American political disease, Sovietophobia endangers democratic values, distorts budgetary priorities and menaces our national security by enhancing the prospect of nuclear war. Its symptoms include militarized thinking about American-Soviet relations, alarmist assertions about Soviet intentions and capabilities and baseless claims that the United States is imperiled by strategic "gaps."

After a brief remission in the 1960s and eaṛly 1970s, Sovietophobia re-emerged by the early 1980s in a form more dangerous than the original cold war epidemic. It was the little-discussed political factor behind the first Reagan Administration's shift from nuclear deterrence to a "nuclear warfighting" strategy, its extravagant defense budget and its farfetched idea for a missile-immunity system. Public debate focused myopically on the financial and technological merits of these radical military proposals; the real issue should have been the ominous change in their underlying political purpose.

All evidence indicates that the Reagan Administration had abandoned both containment and détente, the political goals that shaped American strategic doctrine since the 1940s, for a very different objective: destroying the Soviet Union as a world power and possibly even its Communist system. That was the meaning of President Reagan's persistent talk about "destabilizing" and "prevailing over" the "evil empire," and his apparent unwillingness to negotiate a strategic arms agreement. It meant a rejection of nuclear parity and a renewed and impossible quest for arms superiority, which is a potentially fatal form of Sovietophobia.

The only cure for such outbursts of Sovietophobia is to recognize it as a pathological rather than healthy response to the Soviet Union. Although the Soviet system is highly repressive at home and a dangerous adversary abroad, not even its most alarming behavior explains extreme American reactions.

The present wave of Sovietophobia began in the late 1970s with claims that the Soviet Union had perfidiously killed détente by building up its military forces and by its invasion of Afghanistan in December 1979. But that military buildup had been expected for years, since it fulfilled the longstanding and loudly proclaimed Soviet goal of achieving strategic parity with the United States. And the invasion of Afghanistan, while indefensible, came well after détente was already in a deep political crisis equally of our own making.

Clearly, there is a discrepancy between American perceptions and Soviet realities. Indeed, Americans have habitually found in the Soviet Union only what they seek. Thus, Stalin's terroristic regime of the 1930s had many American admirers, while Brezhnev's far less repressive one had virtually none. In the 1950s, we exaggerated Soviet economic strength; now, we underestimate it. Sovietophobes insist, against all evidence, that no real improvements have occurred in the Soviet system since Stalin, or they turn such changes as have occurred into new indictments. Thus, Soviet leaders are not commended for allowing 260,000 Jews to emigrate since 1971, only condemned for not permitting more to leave.

Misperceptions become especially dangerous when linked to interpretations of Soviet foreign policy. Against all logic, the Carter Administration interpreted the invasion of Afghanistan as a march toward the Persian Gulf, on the erroneous premise that the Soviet Union would soon need foreign oil. That worst-case scenario is forgotten, but its consequences live on in our ominously revised strategic doctrines, huge military budget and failure to ratify the SALT II treaty.

What causes such extreme misperceptions of the Soviet Union? Explanations that point to American anti-Communism or lack of knowledge are inadequate. Those factors have not prevented more balanced attitudes and policies toward China and several other Communist countries.

The real source of Sovietophobia is more fundamental:

the United States, unlike most nations, still has not fully acknowledged that, whether we like it or not, the Soviet Union has become a legitimate great power with interests and entitlements in world affairs comparable to our own. Conceding political parity to the Soviet Union leads logically to nuclear agreements based on military parity and to other détente policies. Denying that status leads, as it always has, only to illusory quests for nuclear superiority and related anti-Soviet goals.

President Reagan's initial position was clear: the Soviet Union is "the focus of evil in the modern world" and thus an illegitimate power. But it is unfair and wrong to associate that ideology solely with him or the Republican Party. Hard-line Democrats opposed all aspects of détente throughout the 1970s, including SALT II. The problem is bipartisan, and a change of administrations will not necessarily solve it.

What the United States needs is a candid discussion focusing on the central, almost forbidden question: Are we ready, after three decades of political supremacy, to recognize the Soviet Union as a coequal legitimate power? We have never had this national discussion, partly because those politicians and policy intellectuals who might answer affirmatively in private still fear Sovietophobic charges of "appeasement," "soft on Communism" or worse.

These "opinion makers" should gain courage from the fact that large majorities of Americans have persistently favored strategic arms agreements, despite their dislike of the Soviet Union and susceptibility to political fear-mongering. (A valuable compilation of relevant opinion polls appeared in the summer 1983 issue of *Public Opinion Quar-*

terly.) Indeed, a 1982 Harris poll found that 86 percent of Americans surveyed wanted such an agreement and 83 percent wanted better relations generally with the Soviet Union.

The American people, it seems, are ready to live with the Soviet Union as a superpower. The polls show they want real leadership, not Sovietophobia. If nothing else, all of our present and future candidates for national office should tell us where they stand on both of our Soviet problems.

[April 9, 1983]

The Soviet System: Crisis or Stability?

EVERY GENERATION or so, Western opinion embraces a new myth about the Soviet Union. The current myth is the "failure and crisis" of the Soviet system at home. Or as Flora Lewis concluded in the *New York Times* not long ago, since its creation in 1917 "the Soviet system has had one great success in building military power and has failed its promises in everything else." That view is accepted by a growing number of Americans on the right and the left, including some Sovietologists who should know better.

If this picture of a crisis-ridden Soviet regime tottering on the edge of an abyss were not so dangerous, it could be dismissed as just another piece of passing foolishness. Unfortunately, it underlies the idea, so popular in the Reagan Administration and other influential circles, that an American policy based on a new arms race and all-out economic warfare will destroy the Soviet Union or "bring it to its knees." Critics of that apocalyptic analysis risk being labeled "appeasers" or Soviet "apologists."

Several factors have contributed to the myth of a collapsing Soviet system, once merely a right-wing fantasy. One is an overreaction to wildly exaggerated claims of

Soviet achievements in the 1930s and again after Sputnik was launched in 1957. Another is the mistaken view that current conditions in Poland also exist in the Soviet Union. Yet another is expanded Western press coverage of the Soviet Union since the 1970s, which has focused on the system's internal problems to the exclusion of its strengths.

It is true, to take several well-publicized examples, that Soviet leaders must cope with declining industrial productivity, an unproductive agricultural system, the growing need for foreign currency to pay for huge grain imports and the increasing difficulty of producing oil to earn that currency. However, the following are also true: the Soviet Union's gross national product at least quadrupled between 1950 and 1980; the 1983 harvest was the best in five years; it is cheaper for the Soviet Union to import grain than to produce more; and Soviet oil exports to the West recently rose almost 40 percent.

But the most misleading assertion is that the Soviet Communist system has utterly failed to deliver on its basic domestic promises over the years. Lacking any popular achievements, it is suggested, the system has alienated Soviet citizens to the point of indifference or even rebellion; the government therefore has no consensual relationship with the people, surviving largely or only because of its military might and repressive power.

Nothing I have learned in years of studying and visiting the Soviet Union, and talking with many sober-minded dissidents, truly supports that picture. Nor would we imagine it to be true of other long-lived political systems, which always develop new sources of stability in older national conditions. All stable systems, even ones as repressive as the Soviet Union can be, rest on a social contract between rulers and ruled—some basic promises and expectations fulfilled, or at worst deferred.

What are the basic promises, the ideological meaning, of Soviet Communism at home? As is clear from both the official ideology and officially sponsored public opinion polls, those promises have far less to do with millennial or libertarian aspects of original Marxism than with five more earthly appeals to the Soviet people that have evolved in modern times. At home, Soviet Communism promises national security (the country will never again be defenseless, as it was in 1941), nationalism, law-and-order safeguards against "anarchy" (which many Russians fear), cradle-to-grave welfarism and a better material life for each generation.

Has the Soviet system really "failed" in those commitments? It has fulfilled, or overfulfilled, the promises of national security and law and order. Russian nationalist-patriotic themes have been integrated into official Marxism-Leninism for forty years, and never so firmly as now. Despite important inadequacies and official exaggerations, a comprehensive welfare system now provides free secondary education, health care, pensions and subsidized housing and food for virtually all citizens. And despite widespread privilege, corruption and shortages, and a decline in the growth of consumption in recent years, ordinary citizens live better than ever before. Between 1950 and 1980, for example, per capita real consumption tripled.

Emphasizing the historical costs of those accomplishments, or contrasting Soviet living standards with American ones, is beside the point. What matters politically is that Soviet adults know those standards and welfare provisions did not exist fifty years ago or less, when illiteracy and famine were rampant. Therefore, they regard them as major achievements of the Soviet system, as Communist promises at least partially fulfilled.

On the other hand, historical achievements usually do not satisfy later generations. Rapid upward mobility is no longer common in the Soviet Union and economic stagnation and military expenditures already conflict with higher consumer expectations. These and other problems, including nationalistic sentiments among non-Slavic peoples, alcoholism and negative demographic trends, may one day erode the government's social contract with the people, and hence its stability. But to assume that will happen soon, or must happen, is to underestimate the system's reformist potential and popular support. Even the official conservatism that blocks reform is shared by many Soviet citizens, and thus is another bond between state and society.

A Soviet émigré to the United States recently expressed surprise at the opinion that "almost all Soviet people are anti-Communist and hate Soviet power." In an article in the émigré press, recounting his conversations with many "typical representatives of Soviet people at all levels," he called that view a "self-deception." Instead of dangerously deceiving ourselves about the Soviet Union's "crisis" and what it calls Communism, we should ask why a system with so many problems is so stable. The answer may lead us to wiser and more compassionate policies.

[*August 6–13, 1983*]

The American Media and the Soviet Union

AMERICA'S renewed crusade against the "Soviet threat," from Central America and the Middle East to outer space, has reopened an old question: Do mainstream American newspapers, magazines and television networks, with their collective power to shape public opinion and influence government policy, give concerned citizens a balanced view of the Soviet Union?

Whether purposely or inadvertently, they fail to do so in at least three fundamental ways. The first is through a pattern of media coverage that systematically highlights the negative aspects of the Soviet domestic system while obscuring the positive ones. Soviet crop failures and abuses of political liberties have been the regular focus of American news stories since the early 1970s, but expanded welfare programs and the rising living standard have gone largely unreported.

Nor is the disparity corrected by what passes for informed analysis, even in widely respected publications. Efforts to show both Soviet achievements and failures are exceedingly rare, whereas wholesale vilifications of the Soviet Union appear frequently. A 1982 article in the *Wall Street Journal* by the influential academic Irving Kristol, for example, informed readers that the entire Soviet system is simply a "regime of mafioso types" with "pathological" beliefs and "no popular roots." The problem is not that the opposite is true but that, as a *Washington Post* correspondent returning from Moscow concluded several years ago, "If Americans know anything about the Soviet Union, we probably know what is bad about it."

The second media offense is more subtle. Objective political analysis requires language that is value free. But much American commentary on Soviet affairs employs special political terms that are inherently biased and laden with double standards. Consider a few of them. The United States has a government, security organizations and allies. The Soviet Union, however, has a regime, secret police and satellites. Our leaders are consummate politicians; theirs are wily, cunning or worse. We give the world information and seek influence; they disseminate propaganda and disinformation while seeking expansion and domination.

Obviously, the two systems are not alike, but such prejudicial language is incompatible with fair-minded analysis. In 1982, for example, the C.I.A. reported the existence of 4 million Soviet "forced laborers." The report, based largely on the fact that all Soviet penal inmates must work, was widely and uncritically publicized in the media, sometimes with references to "slave labor." But convicted prisoners in most American penitentiaries must also work. Does that mean we, too, have "forced laborers"?

Finally, there is the media's habit of creating a popular perception that the Soviet Union is guilty of every charge made against it. In recent years, initial newspaper and television reports virtually convicted the Soviet leadership of the following offenses: increasing military spending by an ominous 4 to 5 percent a year; invading Afghanistan in order to seize Persian Gulf oil; attempting to assassinate the Pope; waging chemical warfare ("yellow rain") in Southeast Asia; and destroying what it knew to be a Korean commercial airliner carrying 269 people. Subsequent less-publicized evidence disproved some of those charges and raised serious doubts about the others. Nonetheless, it seems that in the minds of most Americans, the Soviet Union remains guilty of all of them. The result is increased acceptance of cold war policies.

Can anything be done to correct this wicked-witch image of the Soviet Union? People who acknowledge the problem say we need more information to overcome widespread ignorance about complex Soviet realities. Indeed, there is an appalling lack of elementary knowledge about almost everything Soviet, even among educated Americans. A State Department expert thinks, along with President Reagan, that the founding father of the Soviet Union was "Nikolai" Lenin. Too many college students are not certain about which side the Soviet Union fought on in World War II, and most are surprised to learn that talented writers live and publish in that country today.

But knowledge alone will not solve the problem, which has a long history. A growing body of more balanced information about Soviet life has been available since the 1960s. It has had little positive impact on the media or on public opinion. We know a great deal more about the Soviet Union than we do, for example, about China, which receives far more favorable press attention. And no amount of information would prevent a high-level science and technology official in the Reagan Administration,

William Schneider, Jr., from publishing this judgment: "The Soviet state has contributed practically nothing at all to science, culture, art, industry, agriculture, or to any other field of human endeavor."

Clearly, the problem is also American indifference or resistance to balanced information about the Soviet Union. Other countries frequently receive favorable coverage in the media because of America's historical sympathy for them or because of domestic lobbying in their behalf. No such pro-Soviet factors are at work in the United States, while anti-Soviet lobbies stand ever ready to explain away facts that might suggest some improvement in the Soviet system. Thus, in the February 1983 *Commentary,* the eminent intellectual Walter Laqueur wrote: "There are at present in the Soviet Union relatively few political prisoners. . . . This is not because the Soviet Union is a less repressive regime, but on the contrary, because it is repressive *and* effective."

The solution, if there is one, requires not simply new information but old-fashioned American common sense and fairness. Common sense would tell us that the Soviet leadership had no motives for some of its alleged crimes. Fairness would not allow us to defame a nation that has suffered and achieved so much. Both approaches have been lacking in our thinking about Soviet realities. The reason must be embedded in our history and needs. As a historian of American attitudes toward the Soviet Union concluded, "When talking about the U.S.S.R., Americans were really talking about their own nation and themselves."

[*May 12, 1984*]

Media Leaderology

A S THE American and Soviet political systems went through a prolonged process of leadership succession in 1983 and 1984, each country's media tried to explain how the other system chooses a top leader and the significance of the outcome. On balance, the Soviet media did a somewhat better job.

Consider the contradictory conclusions that typified American coverage of the Soviet leadership succession which began with Leonid Brezhnev's death in November 1982. Most newspaper and television reports confidently predicted that Konstantin Chernenko would be the new leader, reasoning that he had been groomed by Brezhnev as heir to the "all-powerful" Communist Party apparatus. No meaningful changes were expected in Soviet policy.

When the victor turned out to be Yuri Andropov, long-time head of the K.G.B., the American media embraced the opposite interpretation: Andropov had been chosen by a "powerful" K.G.B.-military alliance in revolt against the policy immobility of a corrupt and enfeebled Brezhnev-Chernenko party apparatus. Opinion varied as to whether the K.G.B. or the military was the more muscular partner in the takeover, but commentators agreed that

Andropov had quickly solidified power and become a "strongman" leader who would take decisive steps at home and abroad.

Andropov's strongman image—alternately, faintly liberal and thuggish—prevailed right up to his death in February 1984, despite clear signs that he was gravely ill as early as the fall of 1983. Common sense should have suggested that power was flowing from a stricken leader's hands, as would be expected in other political systems. But on the assumption that a Soviet leader must be a virtual dictator, the American media continued to interpret each political development as evidence of Andropov's ever-growing power. Such reports read like a *Saturday Night Live* skit, as in a *New York Times* headline of December 30, 1983: "Andropov's Situation: Ailing, but Politically Stronger."

The aged Chernenko's emergence as Andropov's successor, therefore, also surprised American journalists. Most had favored "strongman" candidates, including some who lacked essential qualifications. Undaunted, the media found yet another explanation for all that happened, and did not happen, after February 1984. The Soviet Union, it was widely reported, had no real leader. Chernenko was said to be "weak" or a figurehead, with power suddenly dispersed among various institutional bosses, such as Foreign Minister Andrei Gromyko.

The media thus contradicted, without explanation or self-criticism, those analyses it presented with equal certainty only months ago. Where was the kingmaking K.G.B., the demand by military and other bosses for strong central leadership, the impotence of Chernenko's party apparatus? Indeed, how did Chernenko become both General Secretary and President in only two months, when it took Andropov seven? Apparently, journalists were simply parroting the Reagan Administration's election-year claim that the absence of a "real" Soviet leader, not its own bellicose policies, was responsible for the total breakdown in arms negotiations.

No one can blame the American media for failing to predict Andropov's victory or Chernenko's. Soviet succession politics is secretive; even professional Sovietologists did little better. But one can fault the media for fixating on rumors instead of presenting informed and coherent perspectives on the Soviet leadership system, which are readily available in Western scholarly literature. There, journalists could learn, for example, that no Soviet leader has ever managed to pick his successor; that every leader since Lenin has needed at least five years to consolidate authority; and that the power of each party leader since Stalin has shrunk progressively due to the growing role of other institutions and oligarchs, and to longstanding conflicts among them.

In comparison, Soviet media coverage of the 1984 American Presidential campaign seemed relatively well-informed and even sophisticated. To be fair, Soviet journalists have important advantages over their American counterparts. Many are trained experts on the United States and are thus more knowledgeable about their subject. And because our succession process is open, they have far greater access to information. On the other hand, they suffer the disadvantage of press censorship, which requires that they at least pay lip service to official stereotypes, including remnants of the lapsed Stalinist dogma

that American elections are meaningless charades between two "monopoly capitalist" puppets who "serve one
master."

Nonetheless, Soviet citizens could easily discern from
their media that the 1984 election campaign was a popular
democratic process of real political importance. The Soviet press reported in considerable detail the long Democratic primaries, the importance of mass blocs of voters
and the heated debate on issues from nuclear weapons to
school prayer and abortion. Indeed, commentators often
simply echoed prevailing trends in the American press, as
when they interpreted polls, explained a "Teflon President," admired Mario Cuomo's speech to the Democratic
Convention and chided Walter Mondale's positions as
"devoid of eccentricity."

In contrast to our media's instant Kremlinology, Soviet
analysis also seemed refreshingly problematic. Having
long insisted that President Reagan's cold war policies
were both responsible for "dangerous" East-West relations and unpopular with "the American people," commentators offered no orthodox or simplistic explanation
for his probable re-election. Some blamed the Democrats
for failing to offer a "well-defined alternative." Others
emphasized the Teflon factor or the "temporary" economic upturn. A few even violated an official taboo
by suggesting that "average Americans" are deeply anti-
Soviet.

Soviet journalists have learned more about our politics,
it seems, than American journalists have learned about
Soviet politics. An additional reason may be that they
have longer memories and thus are more self-critical.

Commenting on the 1984 election, a Moscow television
pundit warned viewers, "We all thought that Carter
would be better than Ford, and Reagan better than Carter.
. . . We were mistaken."

[*September 22, 1984*]

Civic Courage

IKHAIL GORBACHEV'S campaign to bring about
"fundamental changes" in the Soviet system
raises an important question about his chances
of success and about American perceptions of that system.
Having launched a nationwide crusade against "all kinds
of time-servers, careerists and bureaucrats" in the Soviet
establishment, from political and economic life to culture,
he and his allies are calling for the support of "honorable,
conscientious, decent" members of those same elites. But
do such people exist in the party and state bureaucracies
that administer the authoritarian system, or among the
other elites whose officially sanctioned careers have
brought them status and privilege?

Evidently, most American commentators think that
they do not. For many years, media coverage of the Soviet
Union has attributed virtuous qualities almost only to
dissidents, émigrés and would-be émigrés, leaving the impression that the entire Soviet establishment is conformist,
cynical, corrupt or worse. Even otherwise discriminating
commentators regularly dismiss all Soviet political officials as "thugs" or "stooges," Soviet journalists as "cops"
and accepted Soviet writers as "whores." In American

eyes, it seems, no admirable person can work within the Soviet system.

To be both a successful and a decent person—a *poryadochnyi chelovek,* as Russians say admiringly—is exceedingly difficult in the Soviet Union. In a system where there are no effective democratic checks on abuses of power; where local authorities are often capricious; where protesting even petty wrongs can be risky; where decades of scarcity have created zealously guarded privileges; and where there are almost no alternatives to state-approved careers—in such a system a great many people eventually conform for understandable human reasons. Often they become indifferent to or accomplices in corruption, injustice and cover-ups, as is widely reported these days in Soviet newspapers.

And yet, many members of the various Soviet elites do retain their ideals and their civic courage, as it has long been called in Russia. How could it be otherwise in a nation where the word "conscience" has profound meaning, where the official ideology still professes lofty values and where 19 million adults belong to the Communist Party, which must therefore encompass the full range of human nature? Such people are neither dissidents nor abject conformists. They are ambitious, they love their country and they believe in the Soviet system. But they want the system to change in conformity with their own clear sense of right and wrong, and within their limited possibilities, they behave accordingly.

Frequent travelers to the Soviet Union know of numerous examples of admirable conduct by people of authority and official status. More important, their exemplary behavior is a recurrent theme in the best Soviet literature since the 1950s, and even in dissident writings. It is demonstrated by party officials who argue for more enlightened policies and by economic managers who ignore central directives in order to make the system more productive; by journalists and editors who challenge the censorship, and by schoolteachers and principals who defy orthodoxy in order to enrich their students' education; by exalted academicians and celebrated writers who try to help victimized colleagues, and by young professionals who refuse to become informers in return for a promotion.

Political space for doing good deeds inside the system was considerably greater during Khrushchev's de-Stalinization policies than during Brezhnev's conservative reign. In the early 1960s, Len Karpinsky was a national leader of the Young Communist League and a rising party star. By 1975, as a result of advocating democratic reform behind the scenes, his career was in ruins and he was expelled from the party. In the 1960s, Ivan Khudenko, a state official in Kazakhstan, was authorized to organize an experimental alternative to the orthodox collective farm. Having offended powerful local politicians, he was convicted on false charges and, in 1974, died in prison. But those were exceptional cases. The great majority of *poryadochnyi* officials merely grew more cautious and did, as one confided, "what is right, when it is possible."

Now Gorbachev is appealing to their ideals and again raising their hopes. "Civic courage" has become a slogan of the leadership. Boris Yeltsin, an alternate Politburo member and Gorbachev protégé, told the 1986 party congress that he had not criticized political ills at the previous congress because he "clearly lacked sufficient courage." Other high-ranking political and cultural officials are making similar public admissions. Meanwhile, a mini-thaw, or relaxation, of cultural censorship is unfolding. Its main themes, according to Soviet newspapers, are "conscience and decency," as reflected in the titles of three popular plays running in Moscow: *The Cry, Speak—,* and *Dictatorship of Conscience.*

None of this means that a reformation will occur in Soviet officialdom. Clearly, Gorbachev's call for official candor is also a political weapon in his struggle against opposition to his power and policies; outside his personal circle, no one knows his real values and aspirations. Moreover, civic courage is hard to arouse in the Soviet system where, as Gorbachev and his supporters have openly suggested, "toadyism and servility" are rampant and most officials seem to be "virtuosos at playing it safe."

But Americans may wish to ask if the level of civic courage is so much higher in their own system, where the price is so much cheaper. Recently, for example, the White House budget director juggled figures to please his superiors. Astronauts kept silent about safety concerns so as not to lose flight assignments. U.S. senators would not speak out against Administration foreign policies because they worried about not being reelected. And yet, many Americans insist that to be an admirable political or cultural person in the Soviet Union a citizen must break openly with the system, abandoning all hope of a career and risking martyrdom. Rarely, if ever, do we ask so much of ourselves.

[*May 3, 1986*]

II

From Stalin to Gorbachev

Stalin's Legacy

JOSEPH STALIN died more than thirty years ago, on March 5, 1953, but he remains a deeply divisive and potent force in Soviet political life. On every anniversary of Stalin's death, vodka glasses are raised in Soviet households. Many are hoisted in worshipful toasts to the memory of "our great leader who made the Motherland strong." Many others are lifted to rejoice again over the death of "the greatest criminal our country has known."

The Stalin controversy grows out of the dual nature of his long rule, from 1929 to 1953. Pro-Stalin citizens remember the country's towering achievements under his strong leadership: the Soviet Union became an industrial society, defeated the mighty Nazi invader in World War II and rose to rival the United States as a world power. To these people, Stalin will always be the nation's great modernizer, Generalissimo and statesman.

Anti-Stalinists, on the other hand, refuse to forgive the equally towering mountain of his crimes. Stalin's policies created a Soviet holocaust, from the savage collectivization of the peasantry between 1929 and 1933 to the murderous system of police terror that victimized millions of innocent men, women and even children until 1953. At least 20 million Soviet citizens died as a result of those policies. And that is a conservative estimate. Nor does it include millions of unnecessary wartime casualties or the at least 8 million tormented souls who languished in Stalin's labor camps. For anti-Stalinists, "there is no longer any place in our soul for a justification of his evil deeds."

Soviet policy has already undergone two dramatic turnabouts on this bitter controversy since Stalin's death. Three years after speakers at the state funeral eulogized Stalin's "immortal name," Nikita Khrushchev launched an anti-Stalin campaign as part of his reform policies. By the early 1960s, the Khrushchev government had publicly charged Stalin with "monstrous crimes" and "mass repressions," assaulted his once "infallible" leadership, stripped his name from thousands of memorials and removed his body from the Lenin Mausoleum.

But Khrushchev's anti-Stalinism stirred up increasingly powerful opposition in official circles, on the grounds that it created a "negative attitude toward all authority" and "spit on the history of our country." Such sentiments played a large role in Khrushchev's overthrow in 1964 and in the subsequent defamation of his name.

They also help to explain the official rehabilitation of Stalin's reputation, symbolized by the marble bust placed on his grave behind the mausoleum in 1970. By the 1980s, under Leonid Brezhnev, the Stalin years had been restored as a "heroic and positive" era in Soviet history, and Stalin himself, despite some "mistakes" still attributed to him, rehabilitated as a wise national leader and benefactor. Indeed, some Soviet publications have even justified Stalin's mass terror as a necessary "struggle against destructive and nihilistic elements."

The most important byproduct of Stalin's rehabilitation has been the comeback of the Soviet political police, now called the K.G.B. Khrushchev sharply reduced the size and role of the K.G.B., while his exposés of the twenty-year terror left it badly discredited as the agent of Stalin's "monstrous crimes." Under Brezhnev, however, a major effort was made, in a flood of popular fiction, memoirs and films, to restore the K.G.B.'s authority by romanticizing its wartime and foreign operations.

The success of that effort is clear. In 1953, Stalin's successors arrested and executed his longtime police chief, Lavrenty Beria. Thirty years later, Brezhnev's successors made his longtime K.G.B. chief, Yuri Andropov, the new Soviet leader.

These developments do not portend a return to Stalinist terror, but they do make possible a revival of a more despotic form of leadership. Much pro-Stalin sentiment, in officialdom and in society, is a reaction to problems of declining productivity, shortages and bureaucratic corruption, and to the perceived weak leadership of Brezhnev's last years. Such problems cast a nostalgic glow over the Stalin era as a time when there was a "strong boss" and "we did not have such troubles." And they undoubtedly tempt some Soviet leaders to try more draconian solutions, in line with an old Russian tradition that Pushkin called "the charms of the whip," as was suggested by Andropov's brief campaign to instill "discipline" through police harassment of truant workers and bureaucrats.

But the upsurge of pro-Stalinism does not mean that anti-Stalinism is dead. Depleted and aged, the generation that still clings to aspects of power in the Soviet system rose rapidly and traumatically in politics to fill vacancies created by Stalin's terror. The new generation of top officials will have less reason to be silent about Stalin's crimes, but will also be less able to associate themselves with his epic achievements.

Those leaders may find Khrushchev's anti-Stalinism tempting for two reasons. First, the hypercentralized economic system, which no longer works effectively, is the product of the Stalin era. Any fundamental reform of that system will therefore require both official criticism of the Stalinist past and, to overcome conservative opposition, a reformist ideology. And anti-Stalinism remains the only viable ideology of Communist reform, as it was under Khrushchev. If favorable references to him recently in various Soviet journals are an indication, Soviet citizens have not heard the last of the unduly maligned and nearly forgotten Khrushchev.

No less important, historical justice is a moral idea without a statute of limitations. For two decades, truth-telling about Stalin's mountainous crimes has been banished from officialdom and left in the hands of a dwindling band of dissidents. But Soviet leaders know from their experience since Stalin's death that censoring the past causes historical controversy to fester politically. Eventually, they must respond again to the saying, which still circulates in Moscow, "Tell me your opinion about our Stalinist past, and I'll know who you are."

[March 12, 1983]

Khrushchev and Reform from Above

EW POLITICAL LEADERS have been less honored for the good they achieved than Nikita Khrushchev, who led the Soviet Union out of the terror-ridden wasteland of Stalinism. Overthrown by the political elite on October 14, 1964, his entire career was excised from official histories. No Soviet obituary marked his death, at the age of 77, seven years later. And today, Khrushchev is the only former supreme leader about whom nothing candidly favorable can be published in the Soviet Union. Nor has his reputation fared well in the West, where he is remembered mainly as a blustering adversary who once tried to turn Cuba into a Soviet missile base.

But Khrushchev's enduring legacy, which may one day restore him to a place of official honor, is the bold decade-long reformation of the Soviet system that was carried out under his leadership after Stalin's death. What he achieved is often forgotten. Many official crimes of the Stalinist past were publicly condemned, and twenty-five years of mass terror ended. Millions of people were freed from prison camps and exile, while millions who had perished were exonerated so their families could regain full citizenship. Political life became more open and accessible. Censorship was relaxed, official ideology was made less dogmatic and intellectual and cultural activity grew freer. After decades of neglect, the needs of ordinary people—consumer goods, housing and welfare benefits—were given higher priority.

Ultimately, all those changes were limited. They transformed the Soviet political system but never threatened its dictatorial nature. Nonetheless, by 1964 they had cost Khrushchev the support of virtually every power elite. The result was his ouster and defamation, and the onset of eighteen years of conservative rule under Leonid Brezhnev. Legions of neo-Stalinists, in particular, never forgave Khrushchev, seeing in every unwelcome development, from the Prague Spring of 1967–68 to the advent of open dissent inside the Soviet Union itself, the "poison of Khrushchevism."

Many of Khrushchev's reforms were stopped or reversed by his successors, but every official and citizen still benefits from his lasting achievement: the considerable de-Stalinization of the Soviet Union. Indeed, in these times of growing Soviet problems and changing Soviet leadership, Khrushchev's precedent of bold reform from above may be increasingly relevant. It challenges all those Soviet conservatives who insist that the existing system should not or dare not change, as well as those Western cold warriors who maintain that it cannot.

Western observers often argue, for example, that no reform-minded leader can rise to the top of the Soviet system, that only a ruthless despot could impose meaningful changes on the conservative majority of officials and that the official ideology is too rigid and sterile to inspire such policies. Khrushchev's career raises serious doubts about these fatalistic assumptions, which omit, among other things, the unpredictable role of personality.

Few observers, in the West or in the Soviet Union, anticipated Khrushchev's victory over his formidable rivals in the post-Stalin succession struggle of the 1950s. Even fewer imagined that this uneducated, rustic apparatchik, who had risen from coal miner to Politburo member as a result of Stalin's terrorist politics, would become, as Russians say, a *velikii reformator,* a "great reformer." But despite his complex motives and contradictory policies, he became just that, partly in order to use de-Stalinization against opponents more deeply implicated in Stalin's crimes, partly in penitence for his own misdeeds, but mainly because he wanted history to remember him as Nikita the Good, a benevolent ruler who left his country a far better place than he found it.

Moreover, Khrushchev was never a despot or the sole official proponent of reform. Even after 1958, when he added the premiership to his position as party leader, he lacked Stalin's absolute power. His major policies always encountered powerful opposition, even in the Politburo.

He fought back by reviving long-dormant socialist commitments in Soviet ideology: equality, abundance, efficiency and justice. Coupled with anti-Stalinism, those values brought forth eager reformers in every area of Soviet policy. Some gained Khrushchev's ear and overcame his reluctance to go further, as when he decided to liberate the prison camps and to allow publication of Aleksandr Solzhenitsyn's novella about life there. Although only a minority, thousands of such officials fought alongside Khrushchev, achieving far more change in the system than most Western experts had ever thought possible.

Is Khrushchev's example a valid alternative in Soviet politics today, or was it an aberration produced by special circumstances of the 1950s? Certainly, a new reformist leader would face different obstacles at home and abroad. No longer terrorized, officials throughout the system have grown more conservative and more able to thwart change from above. Nor did Khrushchev have to cope with all the superpower burdens taken on by his successors. Internal reform requires, as he understood, a substantial détente with the United States. But no Soviet leader today can be confident that an American President would meet him halfway, as Dwight Eisenhower did Khrushchev.

And yet, evidence persists of a growing reformist mood in official Soviet circles, including the top leadership, in response to the country's worsening economic and social problems. Since Yuri Andropov's death and during the short tenure of Konstantin Chernenko, the hopes of reformers have centered on the political fortunes of younger Politburo members, especially the new leader Mikhail Gorbachev, who began their careers under Khrushchev (not Stalin) and played no role in his overthrow.

Not surprisingly, there have even been persistent signs of a behind-the-scenes struggle, launched by reformers, to rehabilitate Khrushchev's reputation. If those signs continue, we will know that Gorbachev stands behind them, and that he is preparing to risk his future on another program of bold reform from above.

[*October 20, 1984*]

Brezhnev and the Reign of Conservatism

I S THE SOVIET political system capable of internal reforms? No international question is of such visceral
importance to Americans and yet so badly understood. That much was clear, and almost only that much,
from the frenzied media speculation set off, in November
1982, by the death of Leonid Brezhnev and the emergence
of Yuri Andropov as the new Soviet party leader.

Most American commentary fell into one of two opin-
ions, both misconceived, about the prospect of change
after Brezhnev. Either no "meaningful" change was possible because the Soviet dictatorship never changes. Or everything depended on Andropov because all power is con-
centrated at the pinnacle of the Soviet system.

In fact, fundamental changes, for better and for worse,
have occurred throughout Soviet political history. We
may dismiss those changes because they have not led to
democratization. But often they have had life-or-death
significance for Soviet citizens.

The decade of liberalizing reform, or de-Stalinization,
led by Nikita Khrushchev between 1953 and 1964 is relevant today. Though ultimately limited, Khrushchev's reforms improved virtually every aspect of Soviet life. Mass

terror was ended, millions of political prisoners were released, consumer goods and welfare provisions were given
higher official priority, intellectual life was made freer and
the Soviet Union moved a long distance from cold war
toward détente.

But while Khrushchev's policies demonstrated the possibility of reform from above, his ouster revealed two great
obstacles. First, no Soviet leader since Stalin has had dictatorial power inside the top leadership. Nor has any
leader been able to impose policy on the hundreds of high
officials who actually run the vast centralized bureaucracies of the Soviet party-state, and whose representatives
now sit on the Central Committee and even the Politburo.

That bureaucratic officialdom occupies the essential
arena of Soviet politics, where important conflicts over
power and policy are resolved. It overthrew Khrushchev
when his reforms began to threaten centralized control
over the economy in the early 1960s. And it defeated even
the modest economic reforms proposed by the new Brezhnev-Kosygin leadership in 1965. To be effective, a reformist Soviet leader therefore must build a strong reformist
coalition not only in leadership circles but in the officialdom below.

Therein lies the second great obstacle to reform. Soviet
officialdom includes progressive reformers as well as reac-
tionary neo-Stalinists, but it is dominated by profoundly
conservative elites. Their conservatism, the product of
many historical and contemporary factors, makes them
reverential toward the past, defensively proud of the status
quo and fearful that change will bring a worse future.
Moreover, those sentiments probably are shared by most
Soviet citizens. As a Soviet dissident explained in the late

1970s, "We aren't ruled by a Communist, fascist or mafia party but by a status quo party. Therefore, the people support it."

Born in reaction to Khrushchev's "harebrained" reforms, Brezhnev's eighteen-year reign gave full expression to this conservatism. While shunning all the "excesses" of would-be reformers and neo-Stalinists alike, his administration rehabilitated the Stalinist past, restored the authority of the central political, economic and cultural bureaucracies, and gave officials virtual lifetime tenure. The result was Russia's first truly conservative era since the revolution.

But prolonged conservatism often creates the conditions of future reform by allowing social problems to fester. In particular, the Soviet economy now is beset by increasingly serious problems of declining growth, productivity and supplies. Official reformers since Khrushchev have advocated changes in the hypercentralized system of economic planning and control, similar to ones in Eastern Europe, to give more play to market forces and decision-making below. Repeatedly they have been rebuffed and even silenced.

A crucial question raised by the Brezhnev succession was whether conservative officials now see those problems as crisis-like threats to the status quo, as they did in the 1950s, and therefore are ready for more reformist leadership. Some evidence of this began to appear in official publications even before Brezhnev's death. And the ongoing market reforms in China may offset longstanding conservative objections that such policies are safe only in small Communist countries like Hungary.

Whether Andropov was the man to push through reform is a different question. Soviet leadership succession is a multi-year process of struggle, not a single event. Western accounts regularly exaggerated Andropov's personal power and underestimated the strength of conservative and neo-Stalinist forces. Georgy Malenkov, for example, was quickly named party and state leader after Stalin's death; he, too, appeared confident at the funeral. But he lost the first post within two weeks and the other two years later. At 68, Andropov was the oldest man ever to become party leader. He did not have time for such a prolonged struggle.

And yet, Andropov seems to have been the most reform-minded senior member of Brezhnev's Politburo, an impression he chose to reinforce cautiously in his first policy speeches as the new General Secretary. Nor did his fifteen-year stint as head of the K.G.B. disqualify him as a potential reformer. Soviet police chiefs, who must understand the limits of control, had become advocates of liberalizing change before. Indeed, Andropov may have been the leader most able to assuage conservative fears of reform. And lest we forget that politicians sometimes rise above their former careers, Khrushchev once was called "the butcher of the Ukraine" for his part in Stalin's terror.

Nor should we forget that international affairs always play a large role in struggles between Soviet conservatives and reformers. On at least five critical occasions since 1917, proponents of more liberal domestic policy suffered major defeats inside Soviet officialdom. At each turning point, the Soviet Union felt threatened in its relations with the West.

The lesson is that whereas American hard-liners insist

cold war pressure will force Soviet leaders to reform the system, history tells us otherwise. As Casey Stengel used to say, you could look it up.

[*December 18, 1982*]

Andropov's "Reform"

FOR THIRTY YEARS, every Soviet leader has tried to institute significant reforms in the hypercentralized system of economic planning and management inherited from Stalin. Each has been defeated by conservative forces, particularly the vast and powerful state bureaucracy which runs the system from Moscow. Shortly after becoming leader, Yuri Andropov moved in the same reformist direction in the face of equally determined opposition.

On July 26, 1983, the Andropov leadership, or at least its pro-reform wing, announced a "major economic experiment" that was to take effect the following January. It promised to increase considerably the decision-making authority of plant managers in a few selected industries and regions, and reduce proportionally the role of the central bureaucracy. Three weeks later, Andropov personally declared that "half-measures" could no longer cope with the country's serious economic problems, strongly implying that the reforms would be extended. Nikolai Baibakov, the longtime head of the economic bureaucracy, replied indirectly two days later. He proclaimed the economy healthy, even "dynamic," and suggested that half-measures would be quite adequate.

A confidential Soviet memorandum leaked to Western correspondents in August 1983 was dramatic evidence of the struggle behind those and other oblique polemics. Written by an establishment economic reformer for circulation among high officials, the thirty-page document blamed "the existing state system of economic management" for the sharp drop in productivity since the 1960s. It accused the state bureaucracy of imposing "centralized methods" and irrational decisions, suppressing "market forces" and local initiative and treating plant managers and workers like "cogs." The author of the memorandum called upon the leadership to carry out a "profound" decentralization of the entire "outdated" system.

The secret memorandum belies the notion that no reform movement, or serious political conflict, exists inside Soviet officialdom. Indeed, the extraordinary fact that it was leaked to the Western press, whether by conservatives seeking to discredit reformers or by reformers hoping to force its publication at home, indicates the intensity of the ongoing struggle. But in imploring the leadership to develop "a well-thought-out strategy" to overcome the opposition of bureaucrats whose "warm places" and other "vested interests" are threatened by decentralization, the document raised a critical question reformers probably cannot answer: Even if a Soviet leadership is committed to economic reforms, how can it effect them throughout the bureaucratic system?

No Soviet leader since Stalin has had the power to impose major changes on the state bureaucracy, which has, since the 1960s, sabotaged several reforms in the process of implementing them. Important segments of the

Communist Party, the other administrative bureaucracy, share their counterparts' vested interests. Nor is there any large constituency for change among ordinary citizens, most of whom are deeply conservative, as Soviet pollsters have discovered. Reformers, based mainly in the scientific and cultural intelligentsia, argue that plant managers, technicians and workers want economic decentralization. In reality, most plant bosses and employees probably prefer the existing system, which guarantees superfluous jobs, rewards inefficiency and holds no one personally responsible.

Andropov himself may not actually have wanted "profound" decentralization, but clearly he had a strategy for change. It will be familiar to American politicians. Unlike Nikita Khrushchev, who tied economic change to political and cultural liberalization, and who was overthrown, Andropov linked his economic proposals to two conservative and highly publicized reforms with much larger constituencies.

One was the drive to end the widespread "corruption" associated with Leonid Brezhnev's last years. Such a program has great appeal to ordinary citizens because it promises all-out war on both corrupt officials and crime in the streets, which many Russians resent and fear. The other was Andropov's campaign to "strengthen labor discipline." That appeals strongly to neo-Stalinist bureaucrats, who believe a revival of Stalin's draconian measures against workers, which made even minor workplace infractions a felony, is the way to increase productivity.

Andropov did not live long enough to discover whether those conservative campaigns would have enabled him to build a coalition willing and able to implement significant economic reform. Even though he eventually occupied Brezhnev's former party and state posts, he always had to move cautiously. He made his strongest reform statement, for example, not to a meeting of ranking party or state officials but to a makeshift gathering of aged Communist pensioners. Always invoking the conservative adage "Measure seven times and cut once," he called his economic proposals an "experiment," not a reform, even though they had been discussed and even tested for twenty years. And he allowed Baibakov to chair the commission studying reform, which was like putting the Pentagon chief in charge of Federal budget cuts.

Two other factors will affect the outcome of future bureaucratic struggles over change. Elderly and in poor health, Andropov could not lead a prolonged fight for reform. Only three leaders sat with him as full members on both the Politburo and the Secretariat. The two youngest, Mikhail Gorbachev and Grigory Romanov, already had political responsibility for the economy. Reform will ultimately depend on whether they and their generation of officials are friends or foes of change.

The other factor will be the Soviet military establishment, which must consent to economic reforms that eventually will require transferring some of its resources to the consumer sector in return for higher productivity. The military's position remains unclear, but it will depend largely on the state of Soviet-American relations. Viewed in that context, Andropov's obvious desire for an arms control agreement with the Reagan Administration was not surprising.

[September 17, 1983]

Why There Was No
Andropov Era

WITHIN A YEAR after Yuri Andropov succeeded Leonid Brezhnev as Soviet leader, and well before his death, it was already clear that the "Andropov Era" so widely heralded in the Western press would not unfold.

Most Western commentators predicted that after the growing problems and weak leadership of Brezhnev's last years, Andropov would become a "strongman," perhaps even ruling through the K.G.B., which he headed for fifteen years, and would change Soviet domestic and foreign policy in significant ways. Some initial developments under Andropov seemed to support that expectation: new high-level appointments; more energetic diplomatic overtures toward China and the United States, and toward a resolution of the war in Afghanistan; a surge of reformist rhetoric in the central press; and highly publicized campaigns to fight official corruption, restore "labor discipline" and increase the authority of plant managers.

But after a year, little had changed, certainly far less than during the first year of Khrushchev's or Brezhnev's leadership. Andropov's three domestic campaigns seemed to be petering out, while the Soviet press lapsed into its more self-satisfied tone. Meanwhile, the Soviet Union remained mired militarily in Afghanistan, deadlocked in negotiations with the Chinese and embroiled in a worsening confrontation with the United States.

Nor did Andropov become a strongman, even though in June 1983 he finally attained the ceremonial office of President. Despite several vacancies, only one new voting member was appointed to the Politburo. It was still composed largely of Brezhnev's people, not Andropov's. The same was true of the hundreds of top bosses who actually run the Soviet system, from Moscow ministers to regional party secretaries. The overwhelming majority remained Brezhnev men, aged symbols of unsolved problems and complacent leadership.

Moreover, Andropov, who sought to contrast himself to the long-enfeebled Brezhnev by being a visibly active leader, virtually disappeared from public life after the Korean airliner catastrophe on September 1, 1983. He did not even appear on the anniversary of the Revolution, on November 5. Unless Andropov was already completely incapacitated, poor health is no explanation. Confronted with foreign policy disasters of the magnitude of the airliner incident, ailing leaders of great states manage at least token appearances to reaffirm their authority. As a result, there was again widespread gossip in Moscow about a forthcoming succession—this time, to Andropov himself.

Thus, whereas we can speak meaningfully of a characteristic Russia of Lenin, Stalin, Khrushchev or even Brezhnev, there was no Andropov's Russia, only persistent signs that there would be none. The reasons involve three little-understood features of Soviet politics today.

First, the office of General Secretary of the Communist

Party, the top leadership position, is not so inherently powerful that its occupant automatically becomes a dictator. It took Andropov's predecessors as General Secretary —Stalin, Khrushchev and Brezhnev—five years or more to achieve supremacy. Moreover, each General Secretary after Stalin had exercised less personal power than his predecessor.

The post was particularly weakened under Brezhnev. Still unnerved by their memories of Stalin's capricious terror and Khrushchev's incessant reorganizations, party, state and military bosses opposed the emergence of another strong leader. Brezhnev acquiesced to that sentiment and based his eighteen-year reign on conservative policies that guaranteed the tenure of those officials, thus enhancing their institutional power. Andropov, therefore, was constrained not simply by the swollen power of the Soviet military, as Washington Sovietologists speculated, but by a more general diffusion of power throughout the system, at the expense of the General Secretary. As the oldest and least healthy man ever to assume the post, Andropov had no chance to revitalize it. Indeed, it is possible he was chosen for that reason.

The second constraint on the leader's power is long-standing policy division in the Soviet political elite. Despite the country's economic problems, for example, Soviet officials are deeply divided among those who believe in muddling through, those who want to restore draconian Stalinist measures and those who urge decentralization. The result has been decades of policy immobilism. Nor is there consensus on international affairs. On the central question of Soviet-American relations, Soviet officials are bitterly split between advocates of cold war with the West as Russia's historical destiny, and proponents of the necessity of détente. Here the result has been decades of erratic policy.

Finally, Andropov's first year was one of relentless confrontations and crises abroad—Poland and Afghanistan, Reagan's anti-Soviet crusade, Lebanon, Central America and the Caribbean. None of them were of Andropov's making, but their result was to redouble every Soviet obstacle to internal change, as international tensions always do. Thus, while American hard-liners insist that cold war is necessary because the Soviet system will never change, their policies make such change almost impossible.

Everything we know about Andropov suggests that he was both reform-minded and politically cautious. Had he lived longer, he might have put his imprint on the Soviet system. Instead, he will be remembered as a transitional figure who opened the door more widely to a younger generation of leaders. Indeed, perhaps the most significant development during Andropov's tenure was the emergence of a new inner circle in charge of government and economic affairs. Composed of Mikhail Gorbachev, Grigory Romanov, Geidar Aliev, Nikolai Ryzhkov and Vladimir Dolgikh, the average age of its members was about 58, a full political generation younger than Brezhnev and Andropov.

Many Western analysts argue that the succession of a new generation of officials throughout the Soviet system will make a major difference in policy. But that generation is also deeply divided between friends and foes of change. And it, too, will inherit a Soviet Union that increasingly resembles the lumbering bureaucratic Russia of weak czars rather than the dynamic leader-dominated "total-itarianism" of Stalin or of Orwell's *1984*.

[*November 19, 1983*]

Chernenko and the Stalin Generation's Last Stand

A HISTORIC POLITICAL and human drama lay behind the selection, in February 1984, of 72-year-old Konstantin Chernenko to succeed Yuri Andropov as Soviet leader. The Stalinist generation of officials—men in their 70s whose careers began in the 1930s—was making a defiant last stand against the ravages of age and against an eager successor generation.

The Politburo that chose Chernenko, the oldest man ever to become General Secretary, reflected the Soviet political system. It was divided between representatives of the Stalinist generation and a younger cohort whose obvious candidate for the top post was 52-year-old Mikhail Gorbachev. Despite having buried two aged leaders, Leonid Brezhnev and Andropov, within fifteen months, the old men prevailed again. Chernenko, who was passed over after Brezhnev's death, in November 1982, won this time because he was their only plausible candidate, the last septuagenarian with the necessary credentials to be General Secretary: full membership on both the Politburo and the Secretariat.

But the choice of Chernenko ramified far beyond the Politburo. Septuagenarians lingered in many top posts

throughout the Soviet system—in the economic ministries, foreign policy establishment, provincial party organizations, academies, cultural bureaucracies and editorial
offices. Gorbachev's victory would have signaled their im-
minent retirement, while Chernenko's renewed their hope
of resisting the ambitions of their younger deputies. That
essential message was conveyed to the nation during Andropov's funeral (which was also Chernenko's corona-
tion), as state television focused on three other Politburo
septuagenarians: Premier Nikolai Tikhonov, 78; Defense
Minister Dmitri Ustinov, 75; and Foreign Minister Andrei
Gromyko, 74.

Attention must be paid to the saga of this extraordinary
political generation, which still clings to office as though
to life itself. It acquired its survival instinct early. Shaped
by the great tragedies and triumphs of the Stalinist 1930s
and 1940s, its leading officials rose with blood on their feet
and heroic national achievements to their credit. Young,
poorly educated and inexperienced, they were thrust into
important positions throughout the system as Stalin's
mass terror swept away their predecessors. (By their early
30s, for example, Chernenko was already a regional party
boss, Ustinov a full minister, and Gromyko Ambassador
to the United States.) Surviving both World War II and
another wave of Stalin's terror, they played a major role
in defeating Germany, rebuilding the Soviet postwar economy and making the Soviet Union a superpower. By the
1960s they had become the ruling elite, from Moscow to
the provinces.

Such experiences made these men zealous defenders of
their historical role and political status, and anxious opponents of any fundamental change. Brezhnev, who became

General Secretary in 1964, at 57, was their true generational leader. Repudiating Nikita Khrushchev's anti-Stalinism and capricious personnel policies, which had offended their sensibilities and threatened their tenure, Brezhnev embraced their slogan, "Stability in Cadres." In practice, it meant that ranking party and state positions became lifetime bureaucratic peerages, a policy that produced a geriatric elite.

But challenges to that elite's right to rule until death were already audible in Moscow when I was living there in 1976. Junior officials recalled privately that Lenin had come to power at 47; Stalin's wartime government had been among the youngest in the world; and Khrushchev had been deposed at 70, ostensibly because of his "advanced age." Opinion was widespread that Brezhnev, enfeebled and almost 70, should retire. A defiant retort came from Brezhnev's deputy on the occasion of his own seventieth birthday: "In our country, 70 is considered only middle-aged." Some Muscovites quipped, only half in jest, "They intend to live to be 140!"

They cannot, of course. Andropov needed kidney dialysis treatment within three months of taking office, and Chernenko died barely a year after having become his successor. Scores of their generation's luminaries have passed from the scene in the 1980s, their heroic services solemnly recited by the survivors in a steady stream of obituaries. Indeed, by design or necessity, the generational transition quickened under Andropov. Supervision of administrative and economic affairs passed to the younger cohort in the Politburo and the Secretariat, while perhaps as many as one-fifth of the provincial party secretaries were retired. Moreover, all signs indicate that Chernenko's election was the result of a generational compromise in the Politburo, with Gorbachev made the number two man. With or without Chernenko's blessing, power was already passing to younger officials throughout the system.

That generational change will be historic, but will it change Soviet policy? Some observers argue that because the younger officials are better educated, more pragmatic and less traumatized by the Stalinist past, they will be more reformist at home and accommodating abroad. The argument has merit, but it is too simplistic.

Every political generation everywhere is divided over the burning issues of its time; each produces its own proponents and opponents of change. The new Soviet leaders will be no different in that respect. Indeed, they are likely to be fully united only on the issue of maintaining the nation's superpower standing, including military parity with the United States, which they inherit. Nor has the Stalinist generation been reckless with Soviet power in the nuclear age. Survivors of terror and war, these men have understood, perhaps better than most of us, history's capacity for sudden disaster. Will their successors have such caution?

Younger Soviet leaders, including Gorbachev, will be different in one important respect. Unable to claim credit for any of the nation's historic achievements, they will have to seek their own. If American policy greets them with reason and restraint, they may well seek that generational destiny in reform at home rather than expanded power abroad.

[*March 17, 1984*]

The Lost Soviet Reform

THE EXTRAORDINARY IMPORTANCE of the economic reforms under way in China is dramatized by their absence in the Soviet Union. Simply put, the Chinese Communist Party has rehabilitated the lost economic alternative to Stalinism, while the Soviet leadership continues to reject that still compelling solution to its own problems. If China's act of historical reclamation succeeds, it could change the face of modern Communism.

In 1921, after three years of imposing centralized controls on economic life, Lenin's government introduced the New Economic Policy. NEP, which established a mixed economy, was the first experiment in market socialism. The Soviet state retained control of large-scale manufacturing and heavy industry, the banking and transportation systems and foreign trade. But peasant agriculture, small manufacturing, service industries and retail trade became the preserves of private enterprise. Profit making and competition were encouraged.

NEP sought to achieve balanced modernization by combining consumerism with production, private incentives with nationalization and the market with flexible state planning. Although the dictatorship of the Commu-

nist Party continued, economic liberalization brought
about a still unequaled degree of liberalization in Soviet
political and cultural life during the 1920s. NEP created
new problems, but by 1926 the country had recovered
from the famine and industrial ruin of 1921. Indeed, the
1920s are still remembered as the "golden era" in Soviet
history.

How NEP would have shaped Soviet Communism remains a controversial question, because the entire market
system was abolished in 1929 by Stalin as "rotten liberal-
ism." In its place, he created the present-day Soviet system
based on virtually complete state ownership of the economy, the suppression of market relations and a hypercentralized apparatus of command-planning and control.
Until Stalin died, in 1953, advocating NEP-like solutions
to Soviet or Eastern European economic problems was
forbidden and exceedingly dangerous.

But the rehabilitation of NEP has been an inexorable
temptation to ruling Communist parties ever since Stalin's
death. Wherever economic reformers have gained influence over policy, they have moved away from the monopolistic Stalinist model and toward a mixed economy
—in Yugoslavia, Poland, Czechoslovakia, Hungary and
even East Germany. Until recently, however, there were
two important holdouts: China and the Soviet Union.

Citing the example of "fraternal" parties in Eastern
Europe and invoking Lenin's authority, Soviet reformers
have urged NEP-like solutions to their own problems
of economic shortages and lagging modernization since
the early 1960s, but to almost no avail. Even a modest
managerial reform in 1965 was undermined by vested
bureaucratic interests and then withdrawn by the leader-

ship after Soviet tanks crushed the reformist Czech government in 1968. The "necessity" for that intervention reinforced the official axiom that "rightist" market reforms may sometimes be politically acceptable in small Communist countries, but never in large peasant ones like the Soviet Union.

Herein lies the ramifying importance of de-Maoization. The Chinese leadership began making economic reforms in 1978, and now it is sponsoring a virtual replica of Lenin's NEP. A large private sector is developing alongside state enterprises; profit incentives and market relations are being encouraged, especially among China's vast peasantry. China's NEP is causing problems similar to those in Russia in the 1920s, including growing income differentials, bureaucratic upheaval and unemployment. But its accomplishments are impressive. The annual growth of agricultural output has doubled and peasant income has tripled.

Nor are the Chinese unaware that they have borrowed the Soviet Union's lost alternative. Economists and historians now openly express deep interest in the Soviet 1920s. Even more remarkable, they have politically rehabilitated the most famous Soviet defender of NEP, Nikolai Bukharin, whom Stalin executed as an "enemy of the people" in 1938. While Bukharin's name still cannot be mentioned in the Soviet press except to epitomize the forbidden "rightist deviation," an American biography of him has been published in China.

The full impact of China's NEP on Soviet politics remains to be seen. Commenting on Chinese developments, ranking Soviet *nepists* have begun to call more insistently for "urgent structural reforms." They were emboldened, in part, by the rise of Yuri Andropov, with whom they were once associated. If Sino-Soviet détente is achieved, and China again becomes a "fraternal country," Soviet reformers will have new arguments against their conservative opposition. China, after all, is an even more populous and potentially unruly country than the Soviet Union. They will also argue that while the Soviet Union now recommends NEP, not its own Stalinist model, to Third World countries, China practices what it preaches.

But achieving even a limited NEP in the Soviet Union —for example, legalizing unofficial urban markets and increasing private plots on collective farms—will involve a major political struggle. Millions of planners, managers, petty officials and workers have job security under the existing system, the equivalent of China's "iron rice bowl," and thus are adamantly opposed to any efficiency-oriented reforms. Some Soviet reformers privately lament, "We may need another strong leader to impose changes, but what if he is a new Stalin?" Moreover, unlike China, the Soviet Union is engaged in a costly and dangerous superpower rivalry, which dissuades its leaders from taking any domestic risks or shifting investment priorities from the military sector.

Nonetheless, China's NEP, which involves many of the same political conflicts, may give Soviet reformers their best chance to challenge the Stalinist economic system since the 1960s. That prospect alone is profoundly ironic. In the 1920s, Soviet Communists liked to say that the missing European revolution was unfolding in China. Now it may be the long-overdue Soviet reform.

[*June 4, 1983*]

Waiting for Gorbachev

UNUSUAL expectations preceded the choice, in March 1985, of 54-year-old Mikhail Gorbachev to replace the late Konstantin Chernenko as Soviet leader. Frustrated by two decades of conservative rule and by almost a decade of aged and infirm leadership, reform-minded Soviet officials throughout the system had long been "waiting for Gorbachev," as reports from Moscow put it.

Rarely, if ever, had Soviet reformers placed their hopes so squarely on one contender in a succession struggle that lay ahead and in which they could play no direct role. They did so out of two widely held convictions.

First, reformers believe that the only solution to the country's economic problems is a fundamental shift toward decentralized management, more incentives for industrial workers and a larger role for private enterprise and other market factors in agriculture and consumer services. Second, they are convinced that such reforms are politically impossible until the lingering Stalinist generation of Soviet leaders, enfeebled men in their 70s who began their careers in the 1930s, is replaced by a vigorous post-Stalin generation that is less tied to the past, better educated and thus more competent to govern in the 1980s.

Equating generational change with policy change, reformers are counting on Gorbachev even though the full extent of his innovative views remains concealed behind the outward conformity of "collective" leadership. In various public and private ways, Gorbachev has indicated a preference for several of their proposals. According to reports, he has even privately expressed interest in Lenin's New Economic Policy, which marketized the entire Soviet economy of the 1920s. Changes of that kind, introduced in Eastern Europe since the 1950s and now under way on a massive scale in China, are the real goal of many Soviet reformers.

But it is Gorbachev's unusual political career that really captivates reformers. With degrees in both law and agronomy, he is, at least formally, the best-educated Soviet leader since the 1920s. More important, his rapid rise to the top has been spectacular in a system where snail-like ascents through the bureaucracy are the custom and where competent 60-year-old officials languish in subordinate posts.

Until 1978, when he was suddenly brought to Moscow to be a national secretary in charge of agriculture, Gorbachev was a little-known party boss in his native province of Stavropol. Within two years he had become, at 49, the youngest full member of the Politburo, whose median membership age was over 70. His range of top-level duties continued to expand during the last years of Leonid Brezhnev and the short reigns of Yuri Andropov and Chernenko, even though responsibility for the chronically ill farm sector had been the ruin of other rising politicians.

Andropov's death, in February 1984, left a leadership

composed almost equally of the Stalinist and post-Stalin generations. The emergence of the septuagenarian Chernenko as the new General Secretary clearly involved a compromise between them that made Gorbachev the second-ranking member of the Secretariat. Full membership on both the Politburo and the Secretariat has always been a prerequisite for becoming General Secretary. Since only one other oligarch, 62-year-old Grigory Romanov, had that qualification, Gorbachev was in a strong position to become the next Soviet leader.

But the risks inherent in the position were almost equal to its powers. Number-two Soviet leaders have fared less well than have American vice presidents. Neither Stalin, Nikita Khrushchev nor Andropov ever occupied the position. And though Brezhnev became Khrushchev's heir apparent, he succeeded only because others had fallen by the wayside and because he supported Khrushchev's overthrow.

Not surprisingly, Gorbachev became the target of rival pretenders and powerful groups with different policy interests. His opponents managed, for example, to downplay his pivotal role at the Central Committee meeting that had selected Chernenko. And he did not even address the Central Committee plenum on agriculture in October 1984, which endorsed policies unlike his own. Anti-Gorbachev forces, it seems, tried to rally behind Romanov, the former party boss of Leningrad. A more conventional and hard-line politician with strong ties to the military-defense industry lobby, Romanov was widely disliked by reformers.

Even if Gorbachev does turn out to be a reform-minded leader, he will not automatically have the power to carry out meaningful economic changes against conservative opposition throughout the system. Unlike American Presidents, every General Secretary has needed several years to consolidate power and to build personal authority. And no Soviet leader since Stalin has been able to impose his personal policies on the Politburo, which has grown into an executive council representing a variety of vested interests, or on the recalcitrant administrative bureaucracy that must implement any policy changes.

Indeed, the Soviet Union is no longer the leader-dominated political system that many observers still imagine it to be. Over the years, the office of General Secretary has grown progressively weaker, an erosion of top executive power perhaps unique among large nations. The question is whether this remarkable trend is a kind of law of diminishing general secretaries that reflects deep structural changes in the Soviet system, or whether it is merely the result of a coincidental succession of ailing leaders, and thus likely to be reversed by the younger, more vigorous Gorbachev. In addition, it is far from clear that Soviet elites actually yearn for a strong leader, as reported in the Western press. Such reports probably mistake grass-roots nostalgia for Stalin, the "strong boss," for elite opinion.

Nor will Gorbachev have the full support of his generation. Because of the aging of the governing elite during Brezhnev's eighteen-year rule, generational conflict has been playing a far greater role in Soviet politics than ever before. But there is no united political generation, in the Soviet Union or elsewhere. Generations may rise to power, but once there they are always divided by conflicting ambitions, values and perspectives on the status quo.

The post-Stalin generation, which found a patron in the

much older Andropov, will be no exception—only more vigorous. A recent Western study found, for example, that Gorbachev's contemporaries at the level of provincial party secretaries, from whom come the next ruling elite, are polarized between those who are "complacent" and those who are "impatient" with existing policy—that is, between conservatives and reformers.

None of this means that another era of reform from above, as occurred under Khrushchev, is impossible. Only that the solution does not lie in generational change alone, and that like the chimerical savior in Beckett's *Waiting for Godot,* the reformer Gorbachev may not come.

[*November 17, 1984, and March 1985*]

The Struggle in Moscow

SIX MONTHS AFTER Mikhail Gorbachev became General Secretary of the Communist Party, most American commentators had concluded that he was already the undisputed master of Soviet power and policy. The real situation was different, as indicated by the Soviet press and by officials in Moscow. Gorbachev was secure as party leader, but his program calling for "deep transformations" in the economic system had encountered stubborn bureaucratic opposition, even, as he admitted, at "top echelons," and his own power to legislate such reforms, much less have them implemented, remained limited.

That the struggle continued should have come as no surprise. Soviet political succession has always been a long drama, never a single act. Every new party leader has needed years of patronage, compromise and coercion to extend his authority over broader policy realms. Above all, the fundamental conflict between reformers and conservatives over the Stalinist economic system is now in its fourth decade. And though every General Secretary since Stalin has tried to carry out significant changes in the structure of the economy, not one has succeeded.

Nor did leadership changes after March 1985 suggest the dominant Gorbachev portrayed in so many Western accounts. Except for Grigory Romanov, his only plausible but very weak rival for the general secretaryship, no one had been removed from the Politburo. Its thirteen voting members still included five aged but influential survivors of the conservative Brezhnev era—among them, Nikolai Tikhonov, the 80-year-old Prime Minister who presided over the government apparatus, which is the center of opposition to economic reform.

As for the other voting members, including four promoted under Gorbachev, there was no reason to assume they were merely his political creatures. Like Gorbachev, several are relatively young, reform-minded men who rose rapidly during the brief reign of Yuri Andropov, from 1982 to 1984. But once promoted, former loyalists often turn out to have ambitions of their own, as Nikita Khrushchev and Leonid Brezhnev discovered.

Moreover, Andrei Gromyko's elevation from Foreign Minister to President should not have been interpreted as a great victory for Gorbachev. The view that Gorbachev kicked him upstairs in order to seize control of foreign policy assumed that Gromyko had monopolized the field and had opposed the new General Secretary. There was no evidence for either assumption. Major foreign policy decisions are made in the Politburo, where Gromyko, who made an unusually personal speech for Gorbachev's candidacy, remained a full member.

Most significant, Gorbachev did not get the ceremonial presidency, which was sought and won by the three preceding party leaders because it gave them head-of-state status in international affairs. His public explanation that he was too busy with domestic problems was nonsense; he had been meeting regularly with visiting foreign leaders and had already arranged summits abroad with François Mitterrand and President Reagan. Some Moscow officials said privately that Gorbachev wanted, instead, the powerful office of Prime Minister. If so, he would have had to wage a major battle to repeal the secret 1964 resolution, adopted by the Central Committee when it ousted Khrushchev, prohibiting party leaders from being head of the government ministries.

Whatever the real backstage politics, an upsurge of oblique polemics in the Soviet press was additional evidence of Gorbachev's limited power. As always happens when the top leadership is divided, longstanding advocates and opponents of change in various policy areas perceived new opportunities or dangers and thus intensified their own efforts. After Gorbachev took office, the press filled with conflicting statements on everything from the Stalinist past to present-day China. On June 21, 1985, for example, *Pravda* published a long commentary condemning market reforms and foreign policy initiatives by Eastern European governments. In July, the equally authoritative *Kommunist* featured two articles defending those developments.

Gorbachev's economic policies were at the center of those conflicts. Hinting at more reforms to come, he called for, by 1987, a restructuring of the entire planning and management system which would sharply reduce the direct control exercised by Moscow planners and ministries over local firms; give enterprise managers considerably more freedom to operate by "economic rather than administrative methods"; and cut drastically the vast middle-level bureaucracy of ministerial agencies as "superfluous links." A nationwide expansion of Andropov's limited 1983 "experiment," the program threatened the positions of countless government officials and aroused strong bureaucratic opposition.

In response, Gorbachev's supporters stepped up their attacks on "the ministerial apparatus." In an *Izvestiia* interview on June 1, 1985, the well-known reformer Tatyana Zaslavskaya virtually accused such "group interests"—a fitting but unorthodox pejorative in the Soviet Union—of sabotaging Gorbachev's policy. And in a remarkably candid speech on June 11, Gorbachev personally dropped the customary fiction of a united Soviet leadership. "The ministries," he charged, "have no interest in the economic experiment . . . in the introduction of those principles." The ministries have representatives and allies on the Politburo and Central Committee and are responsible for implementing those principles, so the obstacles to Gorbachev's reforms were, and remain, plentiful.

None of this was new. Twenty years earlier, the fledgling Brezhnev-Kosygin leadership introduced a similar reform with equal fanfare. It disappeared in the government bureaucracy—as Gorbachev put it, "nothing . . . left of its principles."

Can Gorbachev therefore never be the reform leader he clearly wishes to be? Although many circumstances remain the same, much has changed in the Soviet system and in the world where it must compete as a superpower.

Given Gorbachev's youth, the lagging Soviet economy and a growing reformist mood among the elite, he may eventually succeed, but not without a long struggle that has only begun.

[*September 14, 1985*]

Soviet Politics Revitalized

AN IMPORTANT BUT little-reported development has occurred in Soviet politics since Mikhail Gorbachev became leader in March 1985. In contrast to the sterile public discourse of the conservative Brezhnev era, vigorous debates are taking place in many areas of policy-making, from economics and personnel selection to culture. Conservative officials remain adamantly opposed to meaningful change, but reformers, once muffled or banished to obscure journals by the complacent dogmas of the Brezhnev leadership, have gained access to authoritative newspapers for their proposals and criticisms of the status quo.

As is clear from growing disputes in the press and from private discussions with officials and informed intellectuals in Moscow, this revitalization of Soviet political life is no less significant than the process of high-level dismissals and appointments. It indicates that a larger struggle between the friends and foes of change is under way throughout the system. And it suggests that the possibility of broad reform may be greater than is commonly believed in the West.

Gorbachev has been the catalyst of the new policy debates. In particular, his calls for more "openness" about the country's longstanding economic problems and for "profound changes" have emboldened reformers to speak out. One wrote in *Izvestiia,* "Now is a wonderful time. Everything that yesterday was said at the family table or in smoking rooms or in narrow circles is now being said openly." That generalization wildly exaggerates the real parameters of permitted debate, but several officials and establishment intellectuals have insisted privately that the limits will continue to expand under Gorbachev. Some of them even foresee a period of "de-Brezhnevization" similar to the far-reaching political discussions and de-Stalinizing reforms of the Khrushchev years.

Most Western observers have ruled out such a possibility by assuming that Gorbachev is committed to achieving higher economic productivity without any kind of liberalization. But liberal Soviet intellectuals are encouraged by what they perceive to be congenial themes in Gorbachev's speeches, as well as by more concrete steps. One is the appointment to crucial posts of officials reputed to be reform-minded or more tolerant, such as Aleksandr Yakovlev, the new head of the Central Committee's propaganda department. Another is the broadening official indictment of the Brezhnev era, signaled in *Pravda* on November 10, 1985, and obviously authorized by Gorbachev.

Whatever the leader's intentions, there is an unavoidable connection between economic and political change in the state-run Soviet system. Consider the increasingly numerous proposals to reduce central planning and increase the autonomy of enterprise managers; to decriminalize the vast market in petty consumer services and trade; and to expand the role of family farms. Even if only partially implemented, such measures would have significant political consequences by diminishing the state's bureaucratic control over millions of economic actors—that is, over society.

Other current proposals also have clear political implications. In an effort to find capable rather than merely obedient managers, for example, the Gorbachev leadership has encouraged several local experiments in electing economic officials. If expanded, as now seems possible, the innovation would directly reduce the traditional appointment powers, or *nomenklatura,* of party bosses at those levels. Indeed, the "electoral principle" could become a precedent for filling other positions of authority.

Moreover, Gorbachev's appeal for openness in economic affairs has already spread to other policy areas. The writer Yevgeny Yevtushenko and the theater director Mark Zakharov have publicly seized the opportunity to demand greater freedom in cultural and intellectual life. As Yevtushenko put it, "Today's long-awaited striving for change for the better in our country gives us profound hopes . . . that non-concealment will become the norm of civic behavior." Other liberal artists and intellectuals have been pressing censorship authorities to approve an array of banned works, including anti-Stalinist novels by two prominent Soviet writers. There are even signs that forbidden political questions about the past may be reopened. For the first time in many years, the central press has published elliptical but startling references to Stalin's terror, while the long proscribed image of Khrushchev, a symbol of liberalization, was shown on state television.

None of those developments should obscure the tenacious resistance to change that has been pervasive in the

Soviet system for decades. Part of it is inertia and general conservative anxiety about anything new. But much of it is militantly self-interested, particularly in response to efforts to reform the economy. State ministries "have no interest in the economic experiment," as Gorbachev has complained, because it threatens their institutional power. Middle-level bureaucrats are opposed to reduced state control, be it economic or cultural, because many of them would become "superfluous," as he has also said. Not all managers actually want more autonomy because it means more responsibility, as reformers are ruefully discovering. And it is unclear how workers, who are accustomed to job security and bonuses regardless of their performance, will respond to Gorbachev's plan to reward the efficient and fire the slothful.

Despite those obstacles, several informed Muscovites believed that Gorbachev would obtain a pro-reform majority in the Politburo and Central Committee at the 27th Communist Party Congress. None of them could explain, however, how he will implement any legislated reforms through the recalcitrant bureaucracy. Pressed for an answer, they sought hope in symbolism, as is so often the case in Soviet political life—in the fact that this first congress under Gorbachev was scheduled to open on February 25, 1986, the thirtieth anniversary of Khrushchev's historic speech to the Twentieth Party Congress, where he suddenly launched his campaign against the Stalinist past.

[*January 18, 1986*]

Gorbachev's Congress

WHETHER BY DESIGN or chance, the 27th Congress of the Soviet Communist Party opened on February 25, 1986, the thirtieth anniversary of Nikita Khrushchev's historic anti-Stalin speech to the 20th Party Congress. Both events had special significance for the generation of officials headed by the 54-year-old Soviet leader, Mikhail Gorbachev. While the 1986 assembly marked their rise to power in the Soviet system, the 1956 meeting was the formative event of their political youth. As a prominent journalist and party intellectual remarked, "We are the children of the 20th Congress."

Party congresses, like all Soviet political institutions, have changed greatly over the years. From 1917 to 1927, a national congress or conference was held every year and was almost always an occasion for heated factional debates and divided voting on major issues. Under Stalin, however, the gatherings were transformed into docile celebrations of official policy. As his power grew more despotic, they became less and less frequent; only two were held between 1939 and his death in 1953. Since 1956, in accord with current party rules, congresses have been convened at least every five years. They are still largely orchestrated by the leadership, but because of Khrushchev's dramatic report on the morning of February 25, 1956, the 20th Party Congress was truly momentous.

Speaking for four hours to a closed session of 1,500 stunned delegates, Khrushchev dealt a devastating blow to the Stalin cult, which had been a secular religion for twenty years. With graphic accounts of torture and execution, he charged Stalin with personal responsibility for decades of "mass terror" and other calamities, including a series of military disasters during World War II. Khrushchev's "secret speech" was never published in the Soviet Union, but it was read at thousands of official meetings across the country and its general contents soon became widely known.

The speech had far-reaching political consequences. As the manifesto of Khrushchev's de-Stalinization program, it legitimized the once-heretical idea of fundamental change in the Soviet system and in the Communist systems of Eastern Europe. Party reformers, who see its healthy ramifications even in the Prague Spring of 1968 and in Kadarism in Hungary today, still call it "one of the most important documents of our century." Inside the Soviet Union, as an unprecedented official admission of past crimes, it generated a torrent of critical thinking and protest from below, including the intellectual and cultural thaw of the 1950s and early 1960s and the dissident movement that came later.

The impact of the 20th Congress on Soviet citizens was traumatic and divisive. Many older people were implicated in the terror or were unshakable in their Stalinist faith. Some of them could not forgive Khrushchev, but others welcomed his revelations as a necessary act of "purification." The effect on Gorbachev's generation, young adults in their 20s, was especially profound. Told that the leader they had been taught to worship as the "Father of the Peoples" was a genocidal tyrant, they too reacted in various ways. The young poet Feliks Chuyev spoke for some in proclaiming, "I never grow tired/ of the call: Put Stalin back/ on the pedestal!"

But a great many young people, bearing no responsibility for the past, experienced a "spiritual revolution." Throughout party and state establishments, they began their careers as anti-Stalinist reformers, rallying to Khrushchev's call for change and inspired by the aroused intelligentsia's credo, "Duty, honor and conscience." Their generational representatives, such as Yevgeny Yevtushenko and Andrei Voznesensky, were among the best and the most daring writers of the thaw.

Now that generation of officials is taking charge of the Soviet system. Unlike party congresses of the conservative Brezhnev era, where almost 90 percent of the Central Committee was reappointed, the 1986 congress saw a 40 percent change in voting members. Many of the new members are men (and a few women) who came of political age in the 1950s. Of course, much has changed in thirty years. During Brezhnev's long reign, anti-Stalinism and reform were officially repudiated and the 20th Congress fell into disfavor. As is clear from the press and from private discussions in Moscow, many members of this generation have been corrupted by career success or hopelessly disillusioned. Some of the brightest are dead, in exile or broken.

But it also seems clear that many "children of the 20th Congress" are still on the scene, even in the party apparatus, and that Gorbachev's rise has rekindled the ideas and hopes of their youth. More than any other group, they are behind the outburst of bold reformist proposals and the flurry of anti-Stalinist themes in the mass media. Indeed, recent publications by Yevtushenko, who in his early fifties is still their political poet laureate, resound with powerful overtones of the thaw, like a bugle summoning his cohorts back into battle.

Can Gorbachev, who began his own career as a Young Communist League official in 1956, be entirely unaffected by what neo-Stalinists label the "poison" of the 20th Congress? As a Soviet leader, he is unique in several respects, but there are striking echoes of Khrushchev in his call for economic decentralization, his attacks on the state bureaucracies, his populist appeals to larger constituencies, his emphasis on the new and the young, and his effort to revive the nation's idealism.

No one in Moscow seemed to expect anything so dramatic at the 27th Party Congress as happened thirty years ago. Even bold advocates of change stressed the lesson of Khrushchev's overthrow: a reform leader must proceed cautiously. But they hoped that Gorbachev would accelerate the new momentum for change by using his first congress to expand his criticism of the Brezhnev era. Many such middle-aged adults hoped, and are still hoping, to recapture something from their youth, or, as Yevtushenko put it in a stirring poem in *Pravda,* "The years that have been sucked dry/ By the just-so-nothing-happens-ists."

[*February 15 and May 1986*]

The Struggle Continues

EVER SINCE Mikhail Gorbachev became Soviet leader in March 1985, most American commentators have continued to overestimate his personal power and underestimate his commitment to domestic reform. Additional confirmation of those misperceptions was provided by events preceding and during the 27th Communist Party Congress, which met from February 25 to March 6, 1986.

In contrast to his three aged and infirm predecessors, Gorbachev has revitalized the office of General Secretary and become a strong, activist leader. But there is no evidence that he has established "an iron grip on power," as is often said. The post-congress Politburo has eleven other voting members. Most owe their careers to Leonid Brezhnev or Yuri Andropov, not to Gorbachev. Several of them may be his reliable allies in various disputes, but few are his unconditional supporters in matters of major policy— where they have exhibited different approaches—or of personnel. Thus, while Gorbachev had the votes to oust Viktor Grishin as Moscow party boss and from the Politburo, he failed in similar moves against Grishin's counterparts in the Ukraine and Kazakhstan, Vladimir Shcherbitsky and Dinmukhamed Kunaev.

All of these Politburo oligarchs have their own networks of clients to promote, so there is no reason to assume, as is usually done, that only Gorbachev benefited
from the mass personnel changes that occurred in other
party and state organizations after he took office. As General Secretary, his patronage is the most extensive but not
a monopoly, as indicated by the composition of the 307-
member Central Committee announced at the congress.
Many of the approximately 125 new voting members have
ties to other powerful politicians, and 60 percent of all
voting members are holdovers from the Brezhnev era, who
are unlikely to be enthusiastic about Gorbachev's de-
Brezhnevization campaigns.

Moreover, Gorbachev and his loyalists have been relatively candid about the persistence of high-level con-
straints on their ability to shape policy, particularly in the
traditionally conservative state ministries. Informing the
congress that "even now the demand for radical change
gets bogged down," Boris Yeltsin, the new Moscow chief,
went further. He admitted that such opposition is also
rooted in "the party Central Committee apparatus as a
whole." Since the General Secretary is head of that apparatus, Yeltsin's revelation cast more doubt on the extent
of Gorbachev's power.

Most American commentators have also concluded
that Gorbachev is not a real reformer—only a "techno-
crat" or even a "neo-Stalinist" determined to increase
economic productivity without market-related measures
or any kind of political/cultural thaw, as occurred under
Khrushchev. Here, too, the evidence suggests otherwise.
Unable to dictate policy and no doubt mindful of Khrush-

chev's fate, Gorbachev has moved cautiously, assuaging conservatives' anxiety with his calls for order and discipline and avoiding dramatic appeals to the liberal intelligentsia. But during his time in office, he has done little to discourage even bold economic reformers in the establishment and, in his keynote speech to the party congress, he did much to encourage them.

Pointedly and repeatedly, Gorbachev spoke the code words and complaints associated with proponents of market-oriented change since the early 1960s. Rejecting "half-measures" as well as "old stereotypes and practices," he called for "radical reforms" and "the boldest steps." He even evoked Lenin's famous speech introducing the New Economic Policy, which marketized large parts of the Soviet economy in the 1920s and remains a model for many radical reformers. Gorbachev's deputy for agriculture did the same, embracing the NEP principle that if market relations grow alongside a predominant state sector, "there is nothing to be afraid of."

More specifically, Gorbachev strongly implied that he supports longstanding reformist proposals, including private enterprise in service industries, "profit-oriented methods" of state management, revisions in fixed prices to reflect consumer demand, a reduction in compulsory collective farm deliveries and an expanded role for family farming. None of this was negated by his emphatic reaffirmation of central planning; reformers have never proposed its abolition, only a combination of "plan and market." In that respect, Gorbachev's speech was the most reformist by a Soviet leader in more than twenty years.

Nor is there reason to believe that he is opposed to some

kind of thaw. Indeed, Gorbachev's period in office has already brought a significant relaxation in political and cultural life. His demand for more candor about economic and social problems has spread quickly to major newspapers, literature, film and the theater. Characteristic themes of the Khrushchev thaw have reappeared, from attacks on official privilege and corruption to criticism of "the gray flood of hack-work" in state-controlled culture. Censorship is being pushed back, however tentatively; in the Soviet system, that is an aspect of political liberalization.

Although Gorbachev's thaw serves his reformist purpose, it is acquiring its own momentum. In a February 1986 interview with the newspaper *Sovetskaya Rossiya,* the poet Andrei Voznesensky insisted, "People are now mature enough to see and read everything." Similarly, long-forbidden political viewpoints are being reasserted. Before a cheering theater audience, the popular writer and bard Bulat Okudzhava assaulted Stalin for "the blood you made flow like water," while a mass-circulation magazine described the Khrushchev era as "positive." Privately, even some high-level officials have predicted a "new cultural spring." Such developments may not improve the treatment of avowed dissidents, but they correspond to the aspirations of millions of Soviet citizens and thus deserve our attention.

It is too early to foresee the contours of the Gorbachev era, or even to be fully confident there will be one. He has restored the general secretaryship as an active leadership position, relegitimized the principle of fundamental change, and created a political atmosphere of reform. But faced with legions of conservative and neo-Stalinist defenders of the status quo, Gorbachev is still far from being the master of power or policy. With the nature of the Soviet system at stake, we may be certain only that the struggle will continue.

[*March 29, 1986*]

III

Victims and Dissidents

Survivors of the Other Holocaust

SURVIVORS OF Nazi concentration camps occupy a special place in our political consciousness and popular culture, as dramatized in April 1983 when more than 14,000 Jewish survivors and their families met in Washington to inaugurate an official Holocaust museum.

Meanwhile, survivors of the concentration camps of Stalin's Gulag, in which a virtual Soviet holocaust was carried out between 1929 and 1953, continue to live in almost total obscurity. If they gathered with their families in Moscow to dedicate an official memorial to that holocaust—Nikita Khrushchev actually proposed such a monument in 1961—the number might be close to 15 million.

By drawing attention to the largely unknown story of the Gulag survivors, I do not wish to equate Nazism and Stalinism, which were different in important ways. Indeed, the Soviet government was both savior and culprit in these events. Whatever its other acts, the Soviet Union saved more European Jews from Nazism than any other country, first by providing sanctuary for hundreds of thousands of Jews fleeing eastward after the German invasion of Poland, in 1939, and then by destroying the Nazi war machine and liberating the death camps in Eastern Europe.

After Stalin's death in 1953, the Soviet government slowly began to free its own concentration camp inmates. The process culminated in a mass liberation of 7 million or more political prisoners after Khrushchev's denunciation of Stalin in February 1956. By summer, homeward-bound survivors, some still skeleton-like and wearing bits of prison garb, had become a familiar sight across the country.

They were survivors in the fullest sense. Unlike the Nazi death camps, the Gulag's first purpose was forced labor; but harsh working conditions and meager rations were often murderous, and the human toll tragic. According to a conservative estimate, at least 12 million prisoners died in the Gulag between 1936 and 1950.

To its credit, the post-Stalin government helped millions of Gulag survivors return to society in the 1950s, providing them with medical care, living quarters, jobs and pensions. While the great majority slipped back into the anonymity of Soviet society, many achieved professional success, and some even played important political roles under Khrushchev.

But many Soviet returnees had the same personal problems as survivors of the Nazi camps. A great number had lost everything during their Gulag years—families, careers and health. Many were psychologically numbed or otherwise impaired. Some lived in constant anxiety, tormented by nightmares and everyday reminders of the Gulag. Some started new families, but refused to discuss the past with them. Often, their children developed attitudes that were characteristic of children of Nazi camp survivors.

The same moral and political questions that Jews asked also obsessed many Soviet survivors: Who had survived, who had not, and why? Who had been responsible for their suffering, and why had no one helped them?

These survivors, however, returned to their own society, where millions of citizens had been direct accomplices in Stalin's terror or its circumstantial beneficiaries. The poet Anna Akhmatova remarked of those people: "Now they are trembling for their names, positions, apartments, dachas. The whole calculation was that no one would return." She added, "Two Russias are eyeball to eyeball —those who were imprisoned and those who put them there."

That conflict became an important aspect of Soviet politics during Khrushchev's de-Stalinization from 1956 to 1964. It surfaced in formal charges made by survivors against high-ranking "hangmen, torturers and informers," in dramatic confrontations between victims and victimizers, and even in Khrushchev's speeches against his opponents in the leadership. The "camp theme" crept persistently into the officially censored press, along with Nuremberg-like questions of criminal responsibility and punishment.

The Soviet government briefly and reluctantly pursued these Nuremberg issues, but the effort did not go beyond the trial and execution of perhaps twenty-five of Stalin's top policemen and the dismissal of a few thousand officials in the mid-1950s. Too many people, including Soviet leaders, were involved. (Would the Bonn government have

gone further on its own?) Moreover, an almost total si-
lence about these issues was imposed on the Soviet press
following the official rehabilitation of the Stalinist past,
which began with Khrushchev's overthrow and continues
in the 1980s.

After Khrushchev's fall, however, some Soviet survivors began to insist more loudly, like Holocaust survivors,
on the need for "memory" about Stalinist crimes. A remarkable number of Gulag victims and their children
became leading dissidents in the late 1960s, including
Aleksandr Solzhenitsyn, Lev Kopelev, Roy and Zhores
Medvedev and Elena Bonner, Andrei Sakharov's wife.
Equally important, a powerful Gulag literature has since
emerged in *samizdat* and in books published abroad—
memoirs, fiction and history written by survivors such as
Evgenia Ginzburg, Varlam Shalamov and Solzhenitsyn.
Its similarities to Holocaust literature are unmistakable.

We haven't heard the last of these themes from inside
the Soviet Union. Intellectuals are still bitterly divided
over the lesson to be learned from the Gulag holocaust: for
Solzhenitsyn, it is the need to abolish the Soviet socialist
system; for Roy Medvedev, the need for socialist reform.
All agree, however, that "memory" of what happened is
"a duty to those who died, to those who survived . . . to
those who will come after us." That alone guarantees the
continuation of uncensored historical writing and political
dissent inside the Soviet Union.

Nor are official circles really deaf to such themes.
Throughout society, and even officialdom itself, many
Gulag victims and their children remain a potential constituency for another combined wave of anti-Stalinist revelations and reform. Imagine how those people, with their

ingrained Soviet habit of reading between the lines, reacted in February 1983 when a leading Soviet newspaper published a Chinese writer's "tragic" story about survivors of Mao's "evil" Cultural Revolution. The editorial introduction was entitled "So That This Does Not Happen Again."

[*May 7, 1983*]

Child of the Revolution

Y EVGENY GNEDIN, child of the Russian Revolution, died in Moscow on August 14, 1983, at the age of 84. Youthful revolutionary idealist, state official, Soviet diplomat in Nazi Germany, victim of Stalin's terror, hopeful survivor and dissident, his remarkable life reflected the cataclysmic political history of twentieth-century Russia. Gnedin's death occasioned no official Soviet obituaries—bureaucratic farewells issued for unbroken and unquestioning service to the state. Instead, a letter of appreciation, written by Moscow friends, traveled slowly westward, as though burdened by its news: "You know who we have lost."

Much about Gnedin surprised people, including the circumstances of his birth. He was born in 1898 in Dresden, Germany, the son of the legendary "Parvus" (Alexander Helphand), who began political life as an influential Russian Marxist and who died in 1924 as a shadowy German financier and government adviser. Separated from Parvus in 1904, Gnedin's Russian mother took her son to Odessa, where he grew up in the tradition of the intelligentsia, a self-described "romantic revolutionary" torn between poetry and politics. He welcomed the Bolshevik victory in 1917, fought briefly on the side of the Reds in the civil war and afterward moved to Moscow. In 1922, his family connections and knowledge of German led him to a position in the Soviet foreign office.

In *Catastrophe and Rebirth,* his confessional memoirs written fifty years later and published abroad, Gnedin laments having identified his youthful idealism so fully with the new Soviet state and thus having served it so uncritically. His official career flourished, not only in the more liberal 1920s, when he headed the trade section and German desk of the foreign office, but even in the dangerous Stalinist 1930s. In 1931, he left diplomatic service for the higher political position of foreign editor of the government newspaper *Izvestiia.* Presumably for that reason, he also joined the Communist Party.

As was true of so many decent people in the Soviet Union and in the West, Gnedin's misgivings about Stalin's brutal policies at home were overshadowed by the rise of Nazi Germany in 1933. Antifascism became his all-consuming cause, specifically the policy of collective security with Western democracies advocated by Maxim Litvinov, Soviet Foreign Minister and Gnedin's personal patron. In 1935, by order of the Politburo, Gnedin was made First Secretary of the Soviet Embassy in Berlin, where for two years he witnessed the secret diplomacy that led to the Nazi-Soviet Pact of 1939 and to World War II. While Litvinov pursued mutual security treaties with England and France, Stalin's private emissaries were already in Berlin with overtures to Hitler.

Meanwhile, almost all of Gnedin's fellow diplomats and journalists were being massacred in Stalin's terror. In 1937, he was recalled to Moscow to serve Litvinov as press chief of the foreign office. His duties included explaining to Western correspondents the Moscow purge trials and the arrests of the old Bolshevik elite. Gnedin's turn came in May 1939, a few days after Vyacheslav Molotov replaced Litvinov as Foreign Minister, and three months before Stalin made his pact with Hitler. Arrest brought a last official distinction: Stalin's police chief, Lavrenty Beria, personally supervised Gnedin's torture.

Millions of Soviet officials disappeared into Stalin's Gulag, but Gnedin's experience was special. Despite repeated torture, he refused to "confess" or to testify falsely against anyone. And while perhaps 95 percent of those arrested in the 1930s perished, he survived sixteen years of prison, forced-labor camps and "eternal" exile. Exonerated and freed in 1955, he attributed his survival to a long process of "spiritual rebirth" in the Gulag and to the tenacious loyalty of his wife and daughter.

Most survivors emerged from the Gulag broken or cynical, but Gnedin remained alive to all the hopes and disappointments of post-Stalinist Russia. Encouraged by Nikita Khrushchev's de-Stalinization, he rejoined the Communist Party and became a regular contributor to the leading official journal of liberal reform, *Novy Mir*. Then, despite the Gulag-bred "fear always in my bones," he was present at the birth of the dissident movement in the late 1960s, signing protests against Stalin's rehabilitation, new arrests and the invasion of Czechoslovakia in 1968. After 1970, he devoted his literary talents to the world of uncensored typescript literature known as *samizdat*, where his memoirs had a great impact on readers. Four years before his death, he resigned from the party, a rare act of protest in the Soviet Union.

But these bare facts do not fully explain the importance of Gnedin to the many Russians, especially the young, who flocked to him in his later years. For them the small, portly, white-haired man, whose almost angelic face bore no trace of bitterness and seemed strikingly younger than his years, was a living remnant of the old intelligentsia, a link to the martyred fathers they had never known and, above all, an exemplar. A young poet wrote, "My poem's hero, Gnedin/Is a model and a marvel. . . . I fasten onto his tale. He teaches me serious business/And I am eager to learn."

Gnedin's tale, told poetically in his memoirs, describes the long process by which he came to feel some personal responsibility for the Stalinist "catastrophe." His theme was the anguished twentieth-century conflict between idealistic ends and evil means. Unlike many Soviet dissidents, Gnedin preached no doctrines. He offered only the example of his own moral rebirth, achieved by "freeing myself from the psychology of the devoted state bureaucrat and dogmatist," and returning to the values of his youth.

Those values—tolerance, justice and personal decency—may be comfortable platitudes in a democratic society, but they remain radical and difficult individual strivings in the Soviet Union. Yevgeny Gnedin adhered to them faithfully for the rest of his life, a rare man even among dissidents. For the many people who gained historical understanding and personal courage from him, the letter from Moscow provides his rightful epitaph: "Without him, it will be harder to live."

[*January 21, 1984*]

The Crisis of Liberal Dissent

WHATEVER HAPPENED TO the Soviet "dissident movement"? In the early and mid-1970s, its importance in the Western press, American foreign policy and even Presidential politics sometimes seemed to rival that of the Soviet government itself. Now, the subject has almost vanished from Western newspapers and politics.

Part of the answer is well known. Arrests—hundreds of them just in the years since 1979—and other forms of police repression have systematically depleted dissident ranks. Most established leaders, and thousands of activists, are in prison or internal exile or have emigrated.

But repression isn't the whole story. The liberal, or human rights, movement, which Western observers mistake for all Soviet dissent, is undergoing a fundamental programmatic crisis that has eroded its political viability almost as much as has the K.G.B. That decline of liberal dissent, dramatized by the disbanding of the Moscow Helsinki Watch Group in September 1982, has been misinterpreted by the Western press as the end of the dissident movement.

In reality, Soviet political dissent has always been an

array of conflicting outlooks and movements ranging from the far left to the far right. And the dissident views that appeal to most ordinary Russians have never been liberal ones, but nationalist ideas espoused by the right wing, including quasifascist groups that probably would form a regime more illiberal than Brezhnev's, Andropov's, Chernenko's or Gorbachev's.

Liberal dissidents gained pre-eminence in the West in the 1970s for reasons that had little to do with their appeal inside the Soviet Union. They had access to foreign correspondents, familiar democratic values, a galaxy of sympathetic personalities and a towering moral spokesman in Andrei Sakharov. No less important, they addressed their protests primarily to Western governments rather than to Soviet officials or fellow citizens.

That Western orientation actually reflected the underlying crisis of liberal Soviet dissidents, which existed even at the height of their importance in American-Soviet relations and which now has deepened. They have no program, or even guiding ideas, for changing the Soviet system.

As was true in czarist Russia, there are only two ways to change a monopolistic, bureaucratic system for the better: mass revolution from below or official reform from above. Like virtually all Soviet dissidents, liberals abhor the prospect of another revolution even more than they dislike the existing government. But those same liberals, having judged Soviet officialdom to be thoroughly illegitimate and repressive, also reject any possibility of reform from above. Therefore, as many liberals now admit, they can offer no "way out" except pleas to the West.

The result is a deep-seated hopelessness among liberals

that cannot be offset by courageous civil rights protests, calls for a "moral stand" or appeals to the West. Open protests lead to prison. Moral resistance leads away from political activity to spiritual concerns. And the West, whose attention span is short, cannot force the Soviet government to change. No wonder liberal activists cannot replenish their depleted ranks, and the favorite toast of those who remain has become "To the success of our hopeless cause."

Other repressed dissident movements, on the right and on the left, however, have avoided the liberal dead end and sustained their vigor by adopting reformist perspectives of one kind or another. Consider, for example, the charms of Gennady Shimanov, the avatar of extreme right-wing dissent in Moscow. Shimanov accuses human rights liberals of "mutiny" against "our state," while they call his despotic, racist, anti-Western ideas "Russian fascism."

Shimanov's ideas appeal to many ordinary citizens and to some high-level officials for two reasons. He accepts the legitimacy of the Soviet state, objecting only to its "false and spent" Communist ideology. He wants a revitalized Soviet power based on the Russian Orthodox religion. Second, unlike most liberal dissidents, Shimanov addresses social problems that afflict both state and society —falling productivity and Russian birthrates, and the related epidemics of cynicism, alcoholism, abortion and divorce. He assures the ruling bureaucracy that an Orthodox Soviet state would bring forth disciplined, productive, sober and family-oriented citizens. However ominous, Shimanov's program is a reformist (and native) "way out."

Left-wing Soviet dissidents also have responded to the

crisis of liberal dissent. There has been a striking growth of underground socialist circles and programmatic journals since the late 1970s. Moreover, they involve a new generation of dissidents in their 20s and 30s.

These new socialist dissidents are democrats and they admire Sakharov. But they conclude from the experience of the 1970s that the liberal movement's emphasis on civil liberties, antisocialism and the West put it "outside" Soviet problems and possibilities. One socialist dissident writes, "Alas, a local Party committee secretary is incomparably closer to the realities of everyday life than Sakharov or the 'Helsinki Watchers.'"

While more conspiratorial than Roy Medvedev, the only famous socialist dissident who has maintained his political views and freedom since the 1960s, most of these new dissidents advocate programs consistent with his gradualist perspective. Medvedev has always insisted, although it has resulted in unfair liberal attacks on his integrity, that liberalization is possible only through "reform from above," especially economic decentralization, and therefore dissidents must propose loyalist programs for "consumers" inside Soviet officialdom.

Of course, socialist dissidents are also unsafe in the Soviet Union. In April 1982, the K.G.B. arrested five young socialists, an event little noted in the West, and it has threatened Medvedev with arrest. Nonetheless, the future of Soviet dissent now lies primarily on the socialist left and the extreme right, not with the liberal movement of the 1970s, because each offers a reformist "way out" to potential consumers in the Soviet Union, rather than in the West.

[*February 12, 1983*]

Roy Medvedev

ROY MEDVEDEV, the renowned nonconformist historian and since the late 1960s a leading Soviet dissident, has been in danger periodically in recent years. At various times, authorities have threatened him with criminal prosecution, while policemen have followed his moves and barred visitors from his Moscow apartment.

Those actions seem designed to force Medvedev, the last major dissident in the Soviet capital, to leave the country. (His twin brother, Zhores, a biochemist and fellow activist, has lived in involuntary exile in London since 1973.) Medvedev has withstood such threats and, unlike many prominent dissidents, has steadfastly refused to emigrate. But given the mood of cold war intolerance in some official circles—revised laws in effect since February 1984 make the dissemination of virtually any information about Soviet life a criminal offense—a showdown could occur at any time. Medvedev could be banished to a remote region of the Soviet Union, cut off from family and friends, who have sustained him since he was deprived of employment in 1971, or even imprisoned.

Medvedev's situation is especially meaningful because

he has been so unfairly defamed by people who should know better. A fiercely independent and honorable man, he has never conformed to popular conceptions of a Soviet dissident. Whereas most liberal activists in the Soviet Union now reject the entire system and socialist idea, Medvedev remains a pro-Soviet, democratic-socialist reformer. And whereas other leading dissidents urged the United States to repudiate détente in the 1970s, he has always protested cold war American policies as well as repressive Soviet behavior at home and abroad.

As a result, many Soviet émigrés, whose political tolerance does not greatly exceed that of their former government, have denounced Medvedev as a "betrayer" or even a K.G.B. agent. The late Senator Henry Jackson once likened him to "certain Jews [who] fronted for Goering, Goebbels and Hitler." And even a few American journalists, who while in Moscow eagerly exploited Medvedev's careful analysis of Soviet affairs, later ungratefully described him as a "conduit" for official Soviet views. There is no evidence for any of those charges.

The real political significance of Medvedev derives from his longstanding role as the most outspoken Soviet advocate of gradual liberalization from above. He believes that such a change—a Moscow Spring that could lead eventually to democratization—might be introduced by the ruling Communist Party, given the right combination of a reform-minded leadership, as existed under Nikita Khrushchev, and a détente-like international climate. Therefore, Medvedev insists that Soviet dissidents should develop and circulate loyal reformist ideas for eventual "consumers" in the party-state elite instead of directing extremist or anti-Soviet appeals to Western governments.

There is, he reasonably argues, no other hopeful prospect for liberal change in Soviet policy.

Born in 1925, Medvedev has had a life shaped by dramatic changes in official policy. His father, a young army officer and Communist Party philosopher, died in Stalin's terror of the late 1930s. The Medvedev brothers served in the Red Army during World War II and then acquired the equivalent of doctoral degrees, but they remained stigmatized politically and professionally as children of an "enemy of the people" until their father was legally exonerated during Khrushchev's de-Stalinization in 1956. That same year, Roy joined the Communist Party; in the 1960s he had a successful career as an editor and department head in research institutions of the prestigious Academy of Pedagogical Sciences.

His life was changed again by Khrushchev's sudden overthrow in 1964 and by the retrograde policies of the Brezhnev-Kosygin leadership. Alarmed by those developments, Medvedev founded a secret typescript magazine of anti-Stalinist and democratic ideas that circulated for seven years among a small group of establishment intellectuals. In 1969, circulation of his monumental indictment of the Stalin era, *Let History Judge,* led to his expulsion from the Communist Party and to a full-time career as a maverick historian and political dissident.

Despite repeated police threats, searches of his apartment and confiscation of his archives, Medvedev has been remarkably prolific in both roles. His historical writings include eight books, the latest, *All Stalin's Men,* having been published in 1984. Though banned in his homeland, they have been widely translated abroad. His dissenting writings on contemporary Soviet affairs are equally numerous. Focusing on abuses of power, the lack of civil liberties, structural inefficiencies and other failings of the system, they present a highly informed, analytical picture of the Soviet Union today and, as in his *On Socialist Democracy,* the most systematic program for liberal reform developed by a dissident writer.

Such reformers, however, have rarely fared well in Russia, where tenacious authoritarian traditions have usually bred political immobilism, extremism or despair. Caught between a repressive leadership and a liberal dissident community that has lost all hope, Medvedev had become a solitary public figure even before his recent troubles.

And yet, he remains unembittered. A ruddy-faced, silver-haired man, professorial in manner, he discusses the attacks on him coming from various quarters with bemused humor and without rancor. He even remains optimistic that reformist views will grow inside the Communist Party and state establishment, especially among officials of the new generation. Thus, the accelerated promotion of some younger officials during Yuri Andropov's brief tenure as leader encouraged Medvedev, while the advent of the septuagenarian Konstantin Chernenko did not.

It is possible, of course, not to share Roy Medvedev's optimistic appraisal of the potential for change within the Soviet system. But anyone who cares about that nation's future, to which our own is so inextricably linked, must admire his courage and be deeply concerned about his fate.

[*April 14, 1984*]

IV

*Cold War Axis and
Nuclear Peril*

The Legacy of World War II

FOR MOST AMERICANS, World War II is a remote and half-forgotten historical event. For Soviet citizens, however, it is the Great Patriotic War and a traumatic experience that ended "only yesterday."

Those different national memories, and the political conflicts they generate, were especially apparent in 1985, which marked the fortieth anniversary of the war's end. In the United States, few commemorations occurred before the traditional V-E Day ceremonies on May 8. In the Soviet Union, a jubilee was already under way in January.

It is a mistake to think, as many Western observers do, that Soviet memories of World War II are prolonged merely by the unending flow of official propaganda. The government has promoted the remembrance, as reflected in more than 15,000 books on the subject and memorials in every town, but the popular emotion is genuine. More than any other event, including the Revolution, the war shaped the Soviet Union as it exists today, as a political system, society and world power. Its legacy endures among citizens because it was an experience of inseparable

—and colossal—tragedy and triumph.

The tragedy began on June 22, 1941, with the massive, unexpected German invasion and the near-total Soviet defeat. After four years of savage fighting from Moscow to Berlin, it culminated in 20 million Soviet deaths, about equally divided between soldiers and civilians. That often cited but little understood statistic means that virtually every family lost one member or more. And it does not include the millions of survivors who were maimed for life.

Nor has the mourning stopped, particularly among women. Displaying worn photographs of their lost sons, aged mothers of soldiers listed only as missing in action (millions are so designated) still haunt veterans' reunions in hope of hearing some word of their fate. And because only 3 percent of men between the ages of 17 and 20 survived the struggle, millions of women of that generation remain unwed and childless; "their loneliness," as *Izvestiia* reported recently, is yet another "terrible echo of the war."

National glory can never compensate for such tragedies, but for most Soviet citizens, final victory gave sacred meaning to their personal losses. In their eyes, it brought three great achievements: the destruction of the Nazi war machine which had conquered the whole of Europe; the creation of the Soviet empire in Eastern Europe which was to guard against another invasion from the West; and the nation's historic rise to great power in world affairs. So popular were those accomplishments that even embittered Russians forgave the Soviet government's misdeeds that had contributed to the catastrophe of 1941, including Stalin's prewar massacre of Red Army officers, his 1939 Pact with Hitler and the general unpreparedness for the German onslaught.

The shared wartime experience of "grandeur and grief," as a Soviet poet characterized it, changed the relationship between the Communist state and the society in fundamental ways. For the Slavic majority at least, the system finally became a truly national one and thus legitimate. But Soviet "Communism" also changed during the "war for the Motherland," as traditional Russian nationalist values overwhelmed revolutionary and internationalist ones in the official ideology.

If nothing else, the war forged a lasting bond between popular and official outlooks on the Soviet Union's overriding purpose at home and abroad. Henceforth, it was to do everything possible to guarantee that the country would never again be caught unprepared by a surprise attack. That alone explains the people's persistent support, despite the sacrifices required of them in everyday life, for the government's obsession with national security, including its hold over Eastern Europe, its constant fear of falling behind in any area of weaponry and the high priority it gives to military expenditures.

The war's legacy also underlies deeply ambivalent Soviet attitudes toward the United States. On the one hand, officials and citizens alike frequently recall warmly the Soviet-American alliance and gratefully acknowledge the United States aid, or Lend-Lease, that accounted for about 4 percent of Soviet gross production between 1941 and 1945. On the other hand, they resent bitterly any American attempt to slight their role in World War II and see it as part of a forty-year effort to deny the Soviet Union its hard-won right to equality in the postwar world.

Perceiving such slights, as they did in the 1984 American-French commemoration of D-Day at Normandy and again during the 1985 anniversary, Soviet officials insist that their struggle was "decisive" in defeating Nazi Germany and "saving world civilization." They argue that the war's major turning points occurred at Moscow, Stalingrad, Kursk and other Soviet battle sites; that until mid-1944, almost 95 percent of all Nazi ground forces were engaged on the eastern front, where Germany suffered 10 million of its total 13.6 million casualties; and that fifty Soviet citizens died for every one American. Even after forty years, no "historical truth" is more important in Soviet minds.

But apart from the need for "eternal vigilance," Soviet officials are not united on the lessons to be learned from World War II, especially as they may apply to the United States. Pro-détente spokesmen still cite the wartime alliance as evidence that improved relations between the two countries are possible. Other officials point no less adamantly to the German invasion as proof that perilous threats always lie in the West. Thus, they responded to President Reagan's anti-Soviet crusade, in the early 1980s, by equating him with Hitler.

Americans outraged by that analogy should consider the Soviet reaction to our own "lessons" of the war. None is more offensive, even to many dissidents and émigrés, than arguments that the Soviet Union is a latter-day replica of Nazi Germany, driven by the same violent cults and insatiable lust for conquest and with whom any serious negotiations are Munich-like acts of "appeasement."

In the nuclear era, such lessons on both sides are as dangerous as World War II concepts of civil defense. Symbolic acts of mutual understanding and memory are needed to dispel them. If the political will could not be found by April 25, 1985, forty years after the day American and Soviet troops met at the Elbe, there is little reason to believe it will ever be found, at arms talks or anywhere else.

[January 26, 1985]

Our Cold Warriors and Theirs

PRESIDENT REAGAN'S 1982 campaign to stop the natural gas pipeline from Siberia to Western Europe typified much that is wrong with American policy toward the Soviet Union. His motive was to "punish" Moscow for its international transgressions and to prevent closer economic ties between our European allies and the Soviet Union. But the real consequence of Reagan's anti-pipeline campaign could have been to affect adversely the most important debate inside the Soviet political establishment: Should the Soviet Union move toward or away from the West?

On one side of this bitter dispute are reform-minded Russians who argue that progress requires more political, economic, scientific and cultural "bridge-building" to the West. On the other are a great many xenophobic Russians, nurtured by the Stalinist experience and a resurgence of traditional nationalism since the 1960s, who see all Western influence as a "cesspool" of corruption and subversion and as the source of the country's problems, from unrest in Poland to falling Slavic birth rates and nonconformist children in the Soviet Union. Espousing a truculent Russophilism, they want to close off the opening to the West, which has been growing larger since Stalin's death in 1953, and return the country to its autarkic ways behind an imperial iron curtain.

This is no peripheral issue; it is a deep-rooted and potentially fateful struggle over the future of the Soviet Union. Echoing nineteenth-century quarrels between Westernizers and Slavophiles, the debate over a Western-oriented or an iron-curtain Russia divides leaders, dissidents and ordinary citizens alike. It underlies a muted controversy inside the political establishment over détente. In popular culture, it pits ancient cults of *Rodina,* or the Motherland, against modernism.

Beneath the surface, the clash is often acrimonious, as I have witnessed repeatedly. Two middle-aged officials, both Communist Party members and neither Jewish, quarreled at a private Moscow gathering. One insisted: "To save us from our own traditions, from people like you, we need more of the West." The other replied: "You and our Zionist scum would sell Russia's soul for Pepsi-Cola."

In the early 1970s, it seemed that the Western orientation would prevail. Despite strong opposition, Khrushchev had knocked a large hole in iron-curtain Stalinism at home and opened cooperative relations with the citadel of the West, the United States. The Brezhnev government, while reversing other Khrushchev policies, pursued that opening to the fuller détente of the 1972 Nixon-Brezhnev accords. Soviet lines to the West seemed firmly laid, including trade, scientific exchanges, emigration and arms talks.

But the Western orientation has suffered a cascade of

foreign and domestic defeats since 1974. The Jackson-Vanik Amendment reduced Soviet-American trade and emigration to a trickle. American grain embargoes, boycotts, technology bans and renewed drives for military superiority displaced first the spirit of SALT II and then the treaty itself. An arc of border crises from Afghanistan and Iran to Eastern Europe, exacerbated by the specter of a Sino-American axis, made Stalin's fortress strategy seem safer to many officials than Brezhnev's bridge-building. Events in the Middle East revived "world Zionism" as an anti-Semitic synonym for everything Western. Poland's economic crisis demonstrated the "perfidy" of Western credits.

By the early 1980s, as a result of those and other shattered "illusions," iron-curtain Russophilism had gained new force in Soviet politics. Entrenched in powerful party, military and K.G.B. organizations, and trumpeted by influential newspapers, it became a clamorous opposition to the whole opening to the West and a potential contender for power. The bridge-building Brezhnev leadership was on the defensive. Foreign Minister Andrei Gromyko expressed its lament and vulnerability in June 1982: "The current American Administration is very successfully blowing up bridges, one after another, that were built over decades."

Reagan's anti-pipeline campaign could have dealt Soviet Westernizers an even worse blow. The 3,500-mile gas line symbolized everything iron-curtain Russophiles despise: a permanent opening to the West, the selling of Russia's treasures for foreign cash and financial dependence on the outside world. Above all, Reagan's campaign undercut the Westernizers' essential argument that stable Soviet-American relations are possible because American anti-Sovietism is merely an electoral tactic always abandoned by latter-day Presidents, such as Nixon, for "businesslike relations." Reagan's willingness to jeopardize the NATO alliance and apply sanctions even against American-owned companies in order to "punish" the Soviet Union proved, Russophiles could argue, that American Sovietophobia is an organic obstacle to a stable opening to the West.

Completion of the European pipeline over American obstructions gave Soviet Westernizers one fallback position—an opening to the West without the United States. That position was encouraged by Western European editorials protesting Reagan's measures and dissenting from his Manichaean view of the "Soviet danger." As Brezhnev emphasized hopefully in September 1982, détente has "deeper roots" in Europe than in America. But given the obsessive importance of the United States in Soviet thinking, that position may not offset growing anti-Western influence in determining power and policy in Moscow.

Should we care about this internal struggle over the Soviet future? Clearly, the American hard line on the pipeline could have fostered a more lasting Western European estrangement from the United States. But there was also a worse prospect. Reagan's crusade "to prevail" on the pipeline issue abetted the political fortunes of the most xenophobic, militaristic, pogrom-minded forces in Soviet politics. A Russia isolated again from the West would be a nuclear superpower driven back upon its most despotic traditions, resentments and anxieties. Such a development would help no one. Its first victims would be what we profess to care about in foreign affairs—human rights, Eastern Europeans and a safe world.

[*October 23, 1982*]

The Specter of Military Communism

A HISTORIC and potentially contagious development, obscured by Western outrage over the repression of Solidarity, has been unfolding in Poland since martial law began on December 13, 1981. For the first time in the history of Soviet-style systems, a Communist Party has been overthrown by its own military.

Communist Party dictatorship has always been the stated first "inalienable principle" of Soviet Marxism-Leninism and its Eastern European offspring. The party's elites, ideology, organization and policies have dominated and shaped those systems.

Until General Wojciech Jaruzelski's army coup in Poland, that principle had been violated only once. Stalin's terror of the late 1930s temporarily reduced the Soviet party to an instrument of his personal dictatorship. But even under Stalin, the Communist Party remained the supreme political institution, unchallenged by the Soviet military, which suffered no less than the party in the terror.

The assumption that Jaruzelski's Military Council of National Salvation was the Communist Party's "proxy" is myopic. The Polish party virtually disappeared as a meaningful political institution, except in Western (and Soviet) press commentaries. It was replaced by army authority at every political level and lost more than 600,000 members. Even the Central Committee's personnel department, the linchpin of the whole party apparatus, was headed by a general.

Nor did the Military Council move to restore party legitimacy. Instead, it embraced every symbol of martial authority and, despite its accusations against Solidarity, blamed the party's long misrule for Poland's economic and political crisis. Trials of party officials conducted by military prosecutors, for example, took place. Polish authorities eventually may create a Potemkin party at Soviet insistence, but real power is in military hands.

That unprecedented development cast the specter of military takeovers, in times of crisis, over all the Communist Party systems of the Soviet empire. Generals may be party members, but bureaucratic elites everywhere stand politically where they sit professionally. Eastern European armies, which already are involved in political administration and are organized to restore internal order as much as to repel NATO forces, represent traditional authoritarian and nationalist outlooks, not Communist ideas. And Poland must have confirmed those armies' perception that party bureaucracies have become inefficient, corrupt and weak-willed.

Indeed, Poland raised the military specter inside the Soviet Union itself, where party leaders have always feared "Bonapartism." Since the 1960s, the Soviet military establishment has grown into a powerful complex, second only to the party. It controls, in addition to armed force, the best human and material resources and a national political-ideological network of its own. Military elites, trained in special academies that favor the children of officers, are more cohesive and probably more competent than the party elites, and are popularly associated with the rising tide of Russian nationalism.

The Soviet Communist Party is far stronger than its Eastern European counterparts and is in no immediate danger of being overthrown. But it has entered a period of unprecedented leadership changes since Brezhnev's death and it faces severe economic problems. Proposed solutions to those problems have already provoked conflict over the military's swollen, and zealously defended, budget.

Until now, the Soviet military has been the party's junior partner, their top leaderships united by cronyism going back to World War II. Poland, and the end of the Brezhnev generation, may make the military less deferential and more eager for full partnership. Indeed, it has already grown bolder in opposing what a Defense Minister labeled the "unpardonable mistake" of military cuts and in criticizing the party's economic management.

No wonder Soviet party leaders seemed uneasy about Poland's military "normalization." They supported Jaruzelski's coup in desperation to avoid the colossal costs of an invasion. As the Polish party vanished, their anxiety became almost pathetic. Jaruzelski had to don civilian clothes when visiting Brezhnev, and the Soviet press still pretends that Poland is governed by the party or "in accord" with its decisions. It was in this context that Brezhnev, accompanied by senior party leaders, made an extraordinary appearance before 500 high-level Soviet military officials on October 27, 1982, and gave an unusual public pledge "to meet all your needs."

Growing military influence will have different political consequences in different Communist countries, and thus for American policy. Given the Polish Army's nationalist identity and its leverage with the Soviet Union, military government remains Poland's only realistic hope for economic reform and some measure of political autonomy. Neither Solidarity nor the Communist Party can govern the country, and the Catholic Church will not. The only alternative is a Soviet occupation.

The American policy of sanctions against Poland's Military Council, though morally satisfying, therefore served no real purpose. It failed to distinguish between the initial crisis state of martial law and the prospect of more conciliatory but long-term military rule, with or without Jaruzelski. An exclusively punitive policy may even undercut that last hope of a more benign military government.

Nothing good can be said, however, about greater military influence in Soviet politics. The consequences would be more cold war policies at home and abroad and still fewer political and economic reforms. Here, too, our punitive policies only make the worse outcome more likely, as Soviet military hard-liners gain strength from our own.

Meanwhile, as the Soviet Communist Party continues its ritualistic practice of military parades on Red Square, it may ponder the meaning of army rule in Poland and recall Marx's prediction of capitalism's ironic demise: To escape crisis, it calls forth its own gravedigger.

[November 20, 1982]

Cold War Mysteries

EVER SINCE the cold war began in 1917, unexpected and mysterious incidents have periodically disrupted East-West relations just as they were improving. Some have been small intrigues, such as the forged "Zinoviev letter," which caused a break in British-Soviet diplomatic ties in 1924. Others have been large human tragedies, such as the destruction of Korean Air Lines Flight 007 and its 269 passengers by a Soviet fighter plane on September 1, 1983, which undermined recent improvements in American-Soviet relations.

The cold war has witnessed other such incidents, each still partly unexplained. In May 1960, for example, a summit meeting between President Dwight Eisenhower and Soviet leader Nikita Khrushchev was abruptly canceled after an American U-2 spy plane was shot down over Sverdlovsk. In September 1964, Khrushchev's plan to visit Bonn and radically improve relations with that government was suddenly aborted by a toxic gas attack on a West German diplomat in the Soviet Union. And in August 1979, Senate ratification of the SALT II treaty was fatally delayed by the "discovery" of a small Soviet brigade in Cuba, which had been there since 1962.

The historical lesson—leaving aside the occasional role played by anti-détente intriguers on both sides—is that impassioned cold war conclusions reached and acted upon immediately after such events, before the mystery unfolds, always turn out to be wrong. Thus, the K.A.L. incident quickly produced dangerous political accusations and consequences in Washington and in Moscow. But we still do not know the full circumstances or causes of that tragedy. Neither the official American version nor the official Soviet version is fully believable. Indeed, both governments are still engaging in cover-ups, including the withholding of much fuller recordings of the sequence of events than the eleven-minute transcript of Soviet transmissions released by the United States.

What is the American government concealing? Most news reports focused on the South Korean airliner. Why was it more than 300 miles off course and over strategically important Soviet territory for two and a half hours? Was it there accidentally, as Washington claimed; in conjunction with a spy mission, as Moscow charged; or to save fuel, as other reports suggested? The question is important but insufficient: not even proof of a spy mission explains or justifies an attack on a commercial airliner.

A more important question was rarely asked: How many American aircraft were in or near that Soviet airspace during the hours preceding the tragedy? The Reagan Administration belatedly admitted the presence of one RC-135 spy plane, but said that it stayed well outside Soviet airspace and left long before the attack. Skepticism is warranted here, given the long history of American overflights and the fact that one RC-135 mission is to test Soviet air defense on alert. Moreover, United States officials conceded that RC-135s "routinely" fly in the area twenty times a month. But a Soviet missile test had been scheduled for the night of the incident. Did several RC-135s therefore move into the general vicinity during a several-hour period, as one source reported?

The Reagan Administration insisted that it was blameless because Soviet air defense could not possibly have confused the Korean 747 jumbo jet with a smaller RC-135. But the most plausible explanation of what happened is that it did, especially if several RC-135s were involved. Everything we know about the Soviet air-defense operation that night indicates ineptitude and confusion. Even Washington admitted that Soviet controllers or pilots initially identified the intruder as an RC-135. Other sources reported that this identification recurs on the unreleased recordings. The evidence suggests that Soviet military authorities thought they were ordering an attack on an RC-135, not a 747 jumbo jet on an illicit mission, as they claim. If so, the United States contributed to the confusion and thus to the tragedy. Indeed, an RC-135 in the area may even have overheard Flight 007's plight and failed to warn it.

Ironically, the Soviet Union seems to be covering up the same explanation, even though it would have diminished Soviet responsibility for the tragedy. Until Marshal Nikolai Ogarkov, then chief of the general staff, laid down the definitive official version at a press conference on September 9, several Soviet statements implied that Flight 007 had been mistaken for an RC-135. Ogarkov emphatically rejected that explanation, insisting that the Soviet defense system had operated flawlessly and that the attack on

Flight 007 "was not done by mistake." Instead, he rested the entire Soviet case on spy charges against the commercial airliner, a callous justification that politically damaged the Soviet Union abroad even more. In short, Soviet authorities, or at least the military, chose to appear evil rather than incompetent.

That bizarre cover-up, probably designed by the military to preserve its image of infallibility, reflected a conflict between Soviet political and military leaders. The K.A.L. incident was an enormous blow to Yuri Andropov's leadership. It undermined his "peace campaign" to keep American missiles out of Europe, stalled the economic reforms he had announced in July and damaged his personal authority. That was evident in two unprecedented developments. The Soviet military, not the Politburo, took charge of public relations about the incident, as dramatized by Ogarkov's extraordinary press conference. (Soon after, Andropov's men began circulating indirect complaints about the military's "inaccuracies.") Meanwhile, Andropov disappeared, making his first public comment on the incident twenty-seven days later, when he finally endorsed the military's cover-up. Moreover, his statement indicated that the entire affair had undercut his argument, against Soviet hard-liners, that better relations with the Reagan Administration were still possible. Such "illusions," he lamented, had been "dispelled."

If the cover-ups in Moscow and Washington persist, Flight 007 will remain another mystery in cold war history. But one lesson is clear. The tragedy should have shattered the myth of infallible military-technological safeguards that is so essential to anti-arms-control lobbies

on both sides. After all, if Soviet radar cannot tell a jumbo
jet from an RC-135 in two and a half hours, will it be able
to distinguish between a Pershing missile launched from
West Germany and a large errant seagull in six minutes?

[*October 22, 1983*]

The Abolition of American Diplomacy

LET 1983 BE REMEMBERED as the year our cold warriors led us, in the name of national security, to the greatest insecurity in the history of American-Soviet relations. The deployment of intermediate-range missiles in Western Europe was an unnecessary and dangerous act. Its immediate consequence was the counterdeployment of Soviet missiles much closer to the United States. Its enduring consequence will be to increase the risk of nuclear war by intensifying mistrust on both sides, undermining fragile safeguards against the use of such weapons and reducing the time in which crucial decisions can be made from hours to minutes.

The only way back from this nuclear Rubicon is to recognize and repudiate the myopic thinking that has led us there. All our underlying national conflicts with the Soviet Union are political in nature, but as a nation we have stopped thinking politically about any of them. Mainstream American thinking about the Soviet Union has become utterly militarized. It focuses only on weapons problems, reasons only in "strategic" doctrines and thus finds only military solutions.

Americans like to say that politics is the resolution of

conflict through bargaining and compromise. In international affairs, it is called political diplomacy. But the United States no longer has any long-term diplomatic policies toward the Soviet Union, only strategic ones. Indeed, whatever coherent policy we do have is shaped not by State Department diplomats but by the Secretary of Defense and the President's so-called national security adviser—officials whose first premise is military.

Still worse, the folly is bipartisan. President Reagan's initial faith in military solutions, rather than political-diplomatic ones, was the culmination of militarized thinking that flourished under President Carter and remains pervasive in the Democratic Party. None of the Democratic front-runners for the 1984 Presidential nomination proposed a truly political solution to any American-Soviet conflict. Huddled around "centrist" positions, their disagreements with the Reagan Administration and among themselves were quarrels over strategic doctrine and the Pentagon's budget. The obsessive counting of warheads has blinded even ardent opponents of the arms race to the lesson of the 1970s, reaffirmed by the breakdown of the Geneva talks in 1983: no arms control agreement is possible or stable without broader political-diplomatic agreements.

The abolition of American diplomacy toward the Soviet Union is reflected in the fifty-year history of its guiding political idea—détente, or the gradual reduction of conflicts through negotiations instead of through military superiority. In 1933, President Roosevelt instituted the first détente policy by establishing diplomatic relations with the Soviet Union. In 1953, President Eisenhower began diplomatic talks that ended American-Soviet confrontations in Austria and Korea. In 1963, President Kennedy called for renewed American-Soviet diplomacy. In 1973, President Nixon's détente policy was still in force. But in 1983, even the word "détente" was profane in American politics, anathema to leaders of both parties who now accept, or fear, the old slander that it is "appeasement."

Détente, however, is the only rational political policy in American-Soviet relations. Consider the alternatives. Hot war will invite mutual destruction because reliable boundaries no longer exist between the use of conventional weapons and a desperate resort to tactical nuclear ones. Cold war has also become irrational, if only because it has entered a historical stage of missile brinkmanship, as we are now witnessing.

All hope for the future, therefore, requires the rehabilitation of American diplomacy and détente. Bipartisan cold warriors rule out that hope, insisting, on the one hand, that the Soviet Union alone "betrayed" détente in the 1970s and, on the other hand, that all diplomatic possibilities have been exhausted. Both contentions are false. The United States helped sabotage détente in the 1970s by violating its political promises to the Soviet Union, including those of most-favored-nation status in trade and credits, ratification of SALT II and a neutralist policy toward China.

Nor have diplomatic approaches to American-Soviet conflicts today been exhausted. Most haven't even been tried. In the Middle East, for example, we have ousted the Soviet Union from negotiations, even though no political settlement is possible without its participation. We should concede a Soviet negotiating role in return for recognition of Israel by Syria and the Palestine Liberation Organization. In the emotional area of Soviet Jewish emigration, our decision to tie it to economic sanctions through the Jackson-Vanik and Stevenson amendments caused the Soviet Union virtually to end that emigration. We should offer to repeal or waive both amendments in return for renewed emigration. In China policy, we have aroused Soviet military anxieties and outraged our former military ally in Taipei by recklessly offering weapons to Beijing. A policy of American friendship but no weapons to either Chinese government might coax a reduction of Soviet forces along the potentially explosive Sino-Soviet border and also placate Taiwan. As for strategic arms control, an American ratification of SALT II and moratorium on European missile deployment probably would bring forth major Soviet concessions in any future talks.

Such political negotiations will never be easy, and some will fail. Nonetheless, there is evidence that the Soviet leadership, faced with serious domestic and foreign problems, is ready for a renewed and comprehensive diplomacy that could include Central America and possibly even Eastern Europe. Moreover, the choice is now stark and fateful: either diplomacy and détente or militarism and missiles. The Soviet government, of course, contributed to the militarization of our present relationship. But it should shame and alarm citizens of democratic America that the main problem today is a failure of American political thinking and leadership, and that as yet no clear remedy is in sight.

[*December 17, 1983*]

Their Cold Warriors and Ours

AFTER THREE YEARS of cold war policies, the Reagan Administration announced that it was offering Moscow a "constructive working relationship," or what used to be called détente. The offer, even if sincere, could have been too late. For the first time since Stalin, there was the prospect of a Soviet leadership devoted to cold war and no longer believing in détente. Such a government would have been the result of a long struggle inside the Soviet political establishment—a struggle in which American policy has played a lamentable role.

Contrary to widespread American assumptions, official Soviet attitudes toward East-West relations have never been monolithic. A deep ideological division has existed between cold warriors and Western-oriented advocates of détente since the 1950s, when Khrushchev abandoned Stalin's Iron Curtain isolationism for an opening to the West based on "peaceful coexistence." Both sides in the conflict, which recalls the nineteenth-century dispute between Russian Westernizers and Slavophiles, have found strong support in official circles. And while every Soviet leadership since Stalin has pursued a Western orientation in foreign policy, it has done so in the face of a formidable cold war lobby. That lobby may eventually prevail, largely because pro-détente arguments are a shambles.

Soviet proponents of détente have always insisted that significant cooperation with the West, particularly with the United States, is necessary to overcome backwardness in economic and other areas; to insure a superpower role in managing world affairs; and to avoid an unconstrained arms race and a nuclear war. The political question has been whether the Soviet leadership could actually rely on the United States to cooperate despite other Soviet international objectives and longstanding American animosity.

In the early 1970s, pro-détente analysts gave the leadership an assurance that became their undoing. They argued that because the Soviet Union had achieved global military and political equality with the West, détente had become an "objective necessity" for the United States. As proof, they pointed to the "businesslike" Soviet policy of Richard Nixon, once America's arch cold warrior.

The Brezhnev leadership clung to that axiom throughout the deepening crisis of détente in the 1970s and even into the 1980s. It reasoned that Jimmy Carter's haphazardly hard-line policy was a temporary aberration and that Ronald Reagan would turn out to be another Nixon. But Reagan's assault on every premise of détente—his crusade against the "evil empire," his campaign to stop the Soviet-European pipeline and his program to regain military superiority—finally "dispelled" any lingering "illusions" in Moscow, as Yuri Andropov put it in August 1983, and with them the "objective necessity" thesis of the pro-détente lobby.

Soviet cold warriors, having always rejected the premises of any Western orientation, were the beneficiaries of that disillusionment. Espousing Russophile and xeno-phobic ideas that go back to czarist and Stalinist days, they insisted that the Soviet Union's rightful "destiny" as a social order and a great power is fortresslike isolation from the West and principled opposition to it. The United States, the epitome of pernicious Western values, isn't a solution to Soviet problems but the cause of them, from crises in Eastern Europe and Afghanistan to political dissent and social ills at home. Moreover, cold warriors argued, the West is inherently anti-Russian, as evidenced by centuries of conspiracies and invasions, and therefore the United States will never accept the prerequisite of détente: Soviet security and parity in world affairs. Reagan, not Nixon, is the real face of America. Thus, for the Soviet Union, cold war is both political virtue and eternal necessity.

Dismissed as crackpot extremism by many leading Soviet officials only a decade earlier, such views now may have seemed cogent and prudent. Cold war ideology became more prevalent in the Soviet press and in popular culture than at any time since Stalin. Not all of it was directly controlled by the leadership, but some of it was. In 1983, the Soviet Union withdrew from arms talks. A catechism of cold war Communism, *The C.I.A. Against the U.S.S.R.,* was reissued (3 million copies) and serialized as orthodox wisdom in once-pro-détente newspapers. Xenophobic, pro-Stalin novelists won coveted prizes. And in February 1984, the leadership authorized an ominous new law against passing "information" to "foreign organizations." Meanwhile, once-outspoken and influential advocates of détente were dispirited and on the defensive.

The importance of that shift in the struggle between Western-oriented and cold war Communism should not be minimized. Soviet foreign and domestic policies were at stake, since the conflict was also between reform and reaction at home. The struggle, of course, was not over. Several important factors sustained the pro-détente lobby, including certain ties with the West that directly benefit Soviet elites, widespread fear of China and the threat of nuclear war.

But other factors, in addition to American policy, were abetting a cold war government in Moscow. One was the rising tide of nationalist sentiment, upon which cold warriors feed. Another was the growing political weight of watchdog institutions that have always promoted a "vigilant" cold war outlook. Still another was the succession of Soviet leadership changes. Even the new leader Mikhail Gorbachev, who will need several years to consolidate power, may think twice about wagering his political fortunes on "illusions" of détente. Indeed, a strong leadership may be tempted to impose a stringent austerity program at home to cope with the country's economic problems, and thus to heed the calls for sacrifice and rigid controls implicit in cold war.

American cold warriors have always denied that such policy divisions exist in the Soviet establishment. Now, dimly perceiving otherwise, they suggest that a cold war Moscow is actually in America's interest because it will divert the Soviet leadership's attention to contingent "iron curtain" areas and away from global rivalry with the United States. That perspective is cynical and perilous. It will mean more repression in the Soviet Union and Eastern Europe, growing East-West mistrust bred by isolation, a permanent arms race and an even greater risk of nuclear war.

[*February 18, 1984*]

The Failure of the Hard Line

PRESIDENT REAGAN'S decision, in 1984, to adopt a more conciliatory policy in American-Soviet relations tacitly confirmed what had long been clear: after a decade of growing influence, the vaunted "hard-line" approach to the Soviet Union had failed completely.

Ever since 1974, when bipartisan hard-liners scored their first anti-détente victories in Congress, they have insisted that a strategy of ideological warfare, military buildup and economic and related sanctions would achieve two purposes. It would enhance American security by forcing the Soviet Union to capitulate on disputed international issues. More ambitiously, it would impose destabilizing political and economic strains on a crisis-prone Soviet system, thereby compelling the leadership to introduce fundamental reforms at home.

In practice, those ideas, which became sporadic policy during the Carter Administration and a strategic crusade under President Reagan, have contributed to the opposite result in both areas. Since the 1970s, the Soviet leadership has responded with its own unyielding policies in world affairs, broadening its war in Afghanistan, boycotting the Los Angeles Olympics, showing even less toleration of change in Eastern Europe and countering the U.S. military buildup and missile deployments. Instead of more national security, the American hard line has given us more international insecurity.

Its consequences inside the Soviet Union have been equally baneful, even where hard-liners promised tangible results. In 1974, more than 20,000 Soviet Jews were allowed to emigrate; a liberal dissident movement was still tolerated in Moscow; and Aleksandr Solzhenitsyn was deported rather than imprisoned. In 1984, fewer than 1,000 Jews were permitted to leave; liberal dissent was crushed, as reflected in the fate of Andrei Sakharov; and Western-sponsored martyrs such as Anatoly Shcharansky were left to languish in labor camps. Instead of internal Soviet reform, the hard line has contributed to political reaction.

Such American policies are inherently counterproductive because they ignore basic truths about the Soviet Union today. Whatever else may be characteristic of Soviet leaders, they are intensely proud of their country's great-power status, achieved only in their lifetime and at enormous cost, and thus they are profoundly resentful of any perceived challenge to its international prestige.

Confronted with assertions of American superiority, preachments about their own "illegitimacy" and "evil" and ultimatums designed to "punish" them, Soviet leaders will always resort to an uncompromising line, regardless of the hardships involved. Despite their longstanding need for an arms control agreement, for example, they walked out of the talks on European missiles in 1983. And since that visceral reaction to American bombast is widespread among officials and ordinary citizens alike, it strengthens, rather than weakens, the leadership's position at home.

The hard-line goal of reforming the Soviet system through relentless cold war, including an uncontrolled arms race, is even more ill-conceived. We may wish for a liberalized outcome, but the United States does not have the wisdom, the power or the right to intervene in internal Soviet politics. Attempts to do so will always cause more harm than good.

Such efforts are doomed partly because they are predicated on wildly exaggerated conceptions of Soviet domestic problems. In reality, the Soviet Union is not in economic crisis; nor is it politically unstable. Moreover, any economic burdens inflicted by our hard-line measures fall directly on ordinary Soviet citizens, not on the governing elite, and are therefore morally unsuitable as American policy.

Above all, every American campaign to impose liberalizing change on the Soviet system actually sabotages that cause by undermining advocates of reform inside the establishment. It discredits their proposals by associating them with foreign sponsorship or *diktat,* thereby redoubling already powerful conservative and often xenophobic opposition. No less important, it contributes to a growing international climate of cold war, whereas Soviet reformers desperately need détente in order to offset conservative anxieties about the political dangers and economic costs of internal change.

Indeed, the conjunction of rising East-West tensions and the defeat of reformers by despotic or conservative groups in the leadership is a recurrent tragedy in Soviet history. At those historical turning points, the result has often been fateful—draconian domestic policies in 1918; the brutal collectivization of the peasantry in 1929; Stalin's great terror in 1936; the return to terroristic practices after World War II; and the end of official de-Stalinization in the 1960s. On the other hand, on the two occasions when official liberalization did prevail, under Lenin in the 1920s and under Khrushchev in the 1950s, détente-like relations were developing between the Soviet Union and the West.

Our hard-liners, typified by the Committee on the Present Danger, remain stubbornly indifferent to those lessons of history, including the ones taught by their own failed policies since the 1970s. Many of them, inside and outside the Reagan Administration, still clamor for extreme cold war measures. They are deaf even to the present-day appeals of reformers in Communist systems from East Berlin to Moscow. As a Hungarian proponent of liberalization warned: "Reforms are needed, and first of all within the Soviet Union. If there is a new cold war, it is acting against any kind of reform."

But the most direct answer to American hard-liners comes from a Soviet reformer, a retired army colonel now working as an official analyst, who gave an anonymous interview to the British journal *Detente*. Asked to comment on the way Western cold warriors emphasize Soviet domestic problems, he replied: "This is really tragic, because we do have internal problems. We need an economic reform. We need to expand human rights in our country and further to develop Soviet democracy. And we can only make headway in tackling our problems under conditions of prolonged detente. We need detente, lots and lots of detente."

[*December 15, 1984*]

Who's Afraid of Gorbachev?

LET IT BE RECORDED that the initial American response to a new Soviet leader promising some kind of reform to his own people was not one of hopeful encouragement but deep alarm.

Underlying that reaction to the rise of Mikhail Gorbachev, in March 1985, was an ominous trend in American policy thinking which has been obscured by the media's trivial focus on his alleged "mastery of public relations." Faced with the first Soviet leader in thirty years who is both reform-minded and vigorous, some Reagan Administration officials and kindred analysts gravely insisted that even a partially reformed Soviet system will represent a far greater threat to American interests around the world. As one Washington Sovietologist put it, "If the Soviet Union proceeds with real economic reform, that is only going to make the Kremlin more competitive in its rivalry with the United States."

Even though Gorbachev faced enormous internal obstacles to any significant reform and was far from having consolidated his power, the prospect was immediately viewed, according to columnists Rowland Evans and Robert Novak, "with chilling seriousness in Washington." A legion of analysts rushed to warn that the new General Secretary will be an exceptionally "dangerous adversary," or, as an American diplomat cried out, "our most formidable opponent in the Kremlin since Lenin." (Evidently, Gorbachev was expected to outdo Stalin.) The message, it seemed, was that the United States must redouble its vigilance because, in Washington's new watchwords, the "free lunch in East-West relations . . . is over."

The thesis that Soviet reform is inimical to American interests has exercised shadowy influence over policy since the beginning of the Reagan Administration. Now out in the open, its invidious implications should not escape scrutiny. Morally, it is blatantly indifferent to the well-being of ordinary Soviet citizens, who might benefit from economic changes and from any liberal ramifications in political life. So much for pious official claims that the United States wishes the Soviet people well.

Politically, it implies that the U.S. government should, in effect, collaborate with Gorbachev's antireform opponents in the Soviet bureaucracy by denying him the better international relations he will need. Indeed, such a policy may have already been in place, as evidenced by the Administration's abrupt rejection of Gorbachev's first diplomatic overture on April 7, 1985. Reagan spokesmen and most media commentators flatly dismissed the proposal as "propaganda" and an "old trick," even though it contained two significant concessions: a unilateral moratorium on deployment of Soviet Euromissiles and a tacit acceptance of American missiles already deployed in Western Europe. The Administration's refusal even to discuss the proposal could only bolster Soviet opponents of both reform and détente.

To lend weight to this American cold war perspective on Soviet reform, two specious historical arguments have been put forth. One is that economic change will actually be bad for Soviet citizens because, according to "experts" cited in the *New York Times,* previous cases have always entailed "a history of intensified repression." Those unnamed authorities apparently know little about Soviet history.

The Soviet Union has experienced two major episodes of economic reform—the New Economic Policy introduced by Lenin in the 1920s and the de-Stalinization policies begun by Khrushchev in the 1950s. Both led to substantial political liberalization, including a sharp curtailment of police repression and a significant increase in intellectual and cultural freedom, or what Soviet citizens nostalgically call a "thaw." Gorbachev may somehow carry out economic reform without that kind of political relaxation, but history suggests otherwise. Moreover, he has already proposed several measures that entail a degree of liberalization—for instance, more local initiative and less censorship of information.

The second historical fallacy maintains that during periods of domestic reform, the Soviet leadership invariably becomes more aggressive and less accommodating abroad. Here, too, the record suggests otherwise. During the reforms of the 1920s, the Soviet government began its first experiment in what later became known as détente, seeking diplomatic relations and trade agreements with capitalist countries it had previously vilified.

Nor was Khrushchev merely a reckless international buccaneer, as he is so often portrayed. His foreign policies were sometimes threatening to the United States, as in

Hungary, Berlin and Cuba. But they included the withdrawal of Soviet troops from Austria in 1955, a doctrine and practice of "peaceful coexistence," the first visit by a Soviet leader to the United States and the 1963 test-ban treaty. Surely, it is more instructive to remember that Khrushchev was both a reformer at home and a founding father, along with President Eisenhower, of modern-day détente in Soviet-American relations.

It is too early to conclude that Gorbachev, if given a chance, will follow a similar course, but the signs are encouraging. In campaigning for power and since becoming General Secretary, he has pointedly associated himself with longstanding reformist ideas and constituencies in the Soviet establishment. Like earlier reformers, he has indicated that such a domestic program requires a relaxation of international tensions to increase nonmilitary expenditures and to counter conservative protests that change is too risky. Hence his statement that better Soviet-American relations are "extremely necessary." Hence his lament over the current "ice age" in those relations, a metaphor that evokes the possibility of a new thaw at home and abroad, and the essential link between them.

The United States therefore must decide whether it is a friend or foe of Soviet reform. A policy of cold war will almost certainly freeze any prospects of a Moscow spring. The alternative is an American response that is open-minded and hopeful, and thus both wise and worthy of a compassionate nation.

[*May 4, 1985*]

Summit Politics

IF THE UNITED STATES had really wanted to improve
political relations with the Soviet Union and end the
nuclear arms race, the Geneva summit meeting between President Reagan and the new Soviet leader Mikhail Gorbachev, in November 1985, could have been a
historic opportunity. The reason is not that the Soviet
Union had suddenly become a benign or likeminded superpower but that, as Gorbachev has made clear repeatedly, his own "foreign policy is an extension of domestic
policy." Simply put, in order to carry out his program of
reform at home, Gorbachev needs détente and arms control abroad.

None of this has been acknowledged by the Reagan
Administration, which seems to have an acute case of cold
war myopia about developments inside the Soviet Union.
Ever since Gorbachev became General Secretary in
March 1985, it has portrayed him mainly as a slicker but
traditional Soviet apparatchik, even a neo-Stalinist, and
his policy statements as nothing but "public relations."
According to Gen. Edward L. Rowny, special adviser to
the President for arms control matters, "Gorbachev is
likely to emulate most of his predecessors and merely

insure continuity." And on October 22, 1985, shortly before the summit, the President said, "We have yet to see a change in fundamental Soviet positions."

In reality, everything indicates that Gorbachev is the first reform-minded Soviet leader since Nikita Khrushchev came to power in the 1950s. Even before taking office, he pointedly identified himself with the reformist wing of the Communist Party, calling for "deep transformations" and "profound changes" in the state economic system. Since taking office, he has outlined a far-reaching decentralization of industrial management and curtailment of ministerial control, while declaring that "more major, important decisions" are still to come. If proposals in *Pravda* and *Izvestiia* are an indication, those decisions may introduce, among other things, a considerably larger role for private enterprise and market relations.

Such reforms will not bring capitalism or democracy to the Soviet Union, but they will, inescapably, entail liberalizing changes in various areas. They may not alter the situation of active dissidents, but they will improve the everyday life of millions of ordinary citizens and, by relaxing the general political atmosphere and specifically censorship, respond to the aspirations of thousands of intellectuals and artists. Gorbachev may even be preparing to pick up Khrushchev's fallen banner of official de-Stalinization. In September, 1985, for example, the poet Yevgeny Yevtushenko, a bellwether of that long-suppressed cause, was allowed to publish prominently two anti-Stalinist statements.

But these internal possibilities stand no chance of being realized without a significant improvement in Soviet-American relations—for two fundamental reasons. First, the economic reforms envisaged by Gorbachev will require major new investments in nondefense sectors, especially consumer-related industries. Given the laggardly rate of Soviet economic growth, such expenditures will be impossible unless military spending can be reduced or at least frozen. And that will require an end to the strategic weapons race, certainly one as costly as Reagan's Star Wars program.

Second, Gorbachev needs détente-like relations with the United States if he is to become any kind of strong reform leader in the deeply conservative Soviet system. He has brought other reform-minded officials into the top leadership, and he has ousted two more important opponents of economic change, former Prime Minister Nikolai Tikhonov and the longtime Gosplan chief Nikolai Baibakov. But he still must overcome widespread objections in the party elite and the state bureaucracy that even modest forms of decentralization and liberalization are too dangerous because of "the growing American threat." Better relations with Western Europe, Japan and China, which the Gorbachev leadership is also promising, cannot alleviate this central concern. In official Soviet eyes, the United States is the source of the political anxiety and of the arms race.

Despite the compelling domestic factors behind Gorbachev's appeals for a "revival of détente," he could not come to the Geneva summit as a "supplicant," as the Soviet press warned repeatedly before the meeting. Though eager to negotiate political and military agreements, Gorbachev had to be "tough," as the American cliché goes, partly because all leaders of great powers must be so, but also because of his special position as the Soviet

Union's youngest and most Westernized leader in sixty years.

Those personal traits, along with Gorbachev's reform program, have aroused resentment among old-line, iron-curtain Soviet conservatives, who have been heard to refer to him derisively as *malchik,* or "the kid," and as "not one of us." Such attitudes no doubt motivated Andrei Gromyko's unusual assurance to the Central Committee gathering that elected Gorbachev: "Comrades, this man has a nice smile, but he's got iron teeth." Nonetheless, if he had been met at Geneva by a more conciliatory President Reagan, particularly on the issue of arms control, Gorbachev could have shown his teeth back home simply by insisting on U.S. recognition of the Soviet Union's right to equal political status in world affairs. Indeed, for Soviet leaders, that has been the symbolic importance of summits since they began during World War II.

Despite the very meager results of the Geneva summit, and subsequent hard-line "anti-Geneva" actions by the Reagan Administration, Gorbachev is still following his domestic imperative that substantially improved U.S.-Soviet relations are "extremely necessary." At stake is not only his personal fate as a reform leader but the political agenda of a new generation of Soviet officials who will govern into the next century. Unable to claim credit for any of the great achievements of the Soviet past, from industrialization and the defeat of Nazi Germany to the nation's rise to superpower, they may well seek their generational destiny in reform at home rather than in more power abroad.

But will the Reagan Administration eventually seize this historic opportunity for a new and possibly lasting détente? If it fails to do so, as seems likely, it will be saying that the United States actually prefers cold war and a nuclear arms race forever—or something even worse.

[*November 9, 1985, and May 1986*]

Gorbachev's Policy Endangered

SINCE THE GENEVA summit in November 1985, a critical dispute over Mikhail Gorbachev's campaign to restore détente and end the arms race with the United States has developed in the Soviet political establishment. An embattled Gorbachev is arguing that his conciliatory policies are "necessitated by new thinking about the nuclear era," while his opponents charge that they are based on "dangerous illusions" about the United States.

The conflict cannot be fully understood without recalling its history. In the early 1980s, the Reagan Administration's anti-Soviet crusade and strategic weapons buildup had badly discredited Soviet proponents of détente-like political negotiations as an important component of national security. For the same reason, Soviet hard-liners, who have always insisted that the United States is bent on strategic supremacy and that therefore only abundant military power can guarantee Soviet security, had gained new influence in high-level circles.

But when Gorbachev became leader, in March 1985, he immediately set himself against that militaristic trend by calling for a "revival of détente." Why he did so is no mystery. Committed to a costly and long-term program of economic reform, he needs arms control to reduce defense spending, and improved relations with Washington to counter conservative protests that domestic change is too risky in times of international tension. Hoping to appeal to a "realistic" wing of the Reagan Administration, including the President, Gorbachev pressed hard for the Geneva summit meeting. Since then, he has repeatedly defended his "new approaches" to Soviet-American relations against "stone-age ways of thinking" that seem to be entrenched in Moscow no less than in Washington.

The crux of Gorbachev's argument is twofold. First, as he told the party congress in February 1986, in the nuclear age no country can "hope to safeguard itself solely with military-technical means. . . . Ensuring security is a political problem, and it can only be resolved by political means." Second, "security can only be mutual"; it cannot be achieved by "caring exclusively for oneself, especially to the detriment of the other side." More pointedly, as he said elsewhere, "there can be no security for the U.S.S.R. without security for the United States."

Gorbachev's reasoning is a tacit repudiation of previous Soviet policies, as some Moscow officials have privately confirmed. By emphasizing political means of national security, he is trying to rehabilitate détente as the highest priority of Soviet foreign policy and implying that the military buildup under Leonid Brezhnev in the 1970s was excessive. His recommendation that the Soviet Union "act in such a way as to give nobody grounds for fears," for example, suggests that the massive Soviet deployment of Euromissiles was a mistake because it provoked the cur-

rent American buildup. Therefore, to achieve serious political negotiations on arms control and even nuclear
disarmament, as Gorbachev proposed in January 1986, the
Soviet Union should make concessions that will lessen
American fears.

And indeed, under Gorbachev's leadership, there have
been a series of remarkable Soviet concessions, including
a unilateral moratorium on nuclear testing and on deployment of Euromissiles; a promise to remove all Soviet missiles from Europe if the United States withdraws its own,
as well as to dismantle rather than relocate those weapons;
and an acceptance of American demands for rigorous on-
site verification of any arms control treaties. Presumably,
Gorbachev believed that such concessions would bring a
positive American response, thereby vindicating his "new
approaches."

Instead, each of them has been abruptly rejected by the
Reagan Administration. Still worse for Gorbachev, since
his meeting with the President, the Administration has
taken a succession of "anti-Geneva" actions. It ordered a
humiliating reduction in the Soviet U.N. mission in New
York, sent U.S. warships into Soviet waters, suggested
that American military measures against Nicaragua and
Libya were related to Soviet support for those countries,
proceeded with its ambitious program of building new
strategic weapons, including a series of nuclear tests, and
threatened to jettison existing arms control treaties at any
time.

Not surprisingly, those "provocations" have redoubled
high-level Soviet opposition to Gorbachev's conciliatory
policies. As indicated by a torrent of veiled polemics in the

press, hard-liners are protesting that the United States is using the summit process to "conceal an intensified quest for military superiority." They demand that the Soviet Union respond not with political overtures but with a renewed military buildup of its own, which is "the greatest guarantee of security." Gorbachev is unnamed but unmistakably indicated in these accusations. On April 13, 1986, after another American nuclear test, the military newspaper *Krasnaya Zvezda* assaulted the "illusions of people who despite facts to the contrary still believed until a few days ago that the U.S. Administration was capable of heeding the voice of reason."

Thus far, Gorbachev has refused to "slam the door" on détente and arms negotiations, but he and his supporters are clearly on the defensive. Since March 1986, he has even had to reply publicly to "numerous letters to the Central Committee," a euphemism for criticism in leadership circles. Denying that he has "the slightest illusions," Gorbachev has pleaded for restraint and promised not to participate in any future summit that is "empty talk" or a "smokescreen" for an American "spurt forward in arms," as his opponents have characterized the one in Geneva.

Much is at stake in this dispute, including Gorbachev's career as a reform leader at home and a historic opportunity to stop the nuclear weapons race. No American can be proud of the fact that there is an imperiled arms-control leadership in Moscow but an unrepentant arms-race government in Washington. Consider their different reactions to the disaster at the Chernobyl nuclear plant in April 1986: while the Reagan Administration could only find more reasons to oppose negotiations, Gorbachev, however lamentable his initial response to the calamity, saw it as "yet another tolling of the bell, yet another terrible warning that the nuclear era demands new political thinking and a new policy."

[*May 31, 1986*]

America's Missing Debate

THE GREATEST FAILURE of American democracy today is the absence of a real national debate on U.S. policy toward the Soviet Union. No international or domestic issue is more important, and nothing in the foreseeable future—including any future summit meetings—will change that fact. In the nuclear age, the nature of the U.S.-Soviet relationship is a matter of global survival. And as government defense-related spending soars toward $400 billion a year, cold war relations increasingly and inescapably erode the quality of American life, from education and Social Security to urban housing and agriculture.

Despite all these ramifications, President Reagan's cold war policy has gone essentially unchallenged in the American political mainstream. Critics have lamented the Administration's extremist rhetoric, protested some of its weapons programs and doubted its commitment to arms control. But not one influential group or institution has mounted a sustained opposition to Reagan's militarized approach to the Soviet Union, either by rejecting its underlying political premises or by offering the only alternative, a broad policy of détente.

As a result, in contrast to wide-ranging controversies over other issues, mainstream discussion of U.S.-Soviet relations is narrow and superficial. It fixates on trivial or secondary matters, such as superpower "public relations" and the efficacy of yet another weapons system, while avoiding fundamental questions about the long-term goal of American policy. Is it to live peacefully with the Soviet Union as an equal superpower? To roll back Soviet power in the world? To destroy the Soviet system? No coherent policy is possible without answers to these and other questions about the kind of relationship the United States wants. They are not even being discussed.

The entire American political spectrum bears responsibility for this failure of the democratic process. The right is mindlessly committed to cold war, including military build-up, as an eternal virtue. The left is instinctively opposed to the arms race but has no ideas for achieving the broader political accords needed to end it. And the vaunted "bipartisan center" wishes only to stand safely somewhere between them.

More specifically, there is the baneful role of the national media, the Democratic Party and the legion of professional foreign policy intellectuals. Each has some capacity, as well as duty, to broaden and deepen public discourse about U.S.-Soviet relations. Not one has done so.

In the 1970s, newspaper editorial pages and network television programs regularly featured proponents and opponents of détente. Now, overwhelmingly, they present only representatives of the cold war right and the center, typically a supporter of the Reagan Administration and a self-described "defense Democrat." In addition, the recent practice, as on ABC's *Nightline,* of casting a Soviet official in the role of primary anti-Reagan spokesman implies that there is no legitimate American position anywhere between them.

The media's culpability may be mostly passive, but nothing so kind can be said about the Democratic Party. Even though Reagan's military expenditures have savaged the party's social programs, it offered no alternative to his Soviet policy in 1984 and seems determined not to do so in future elections. One party politician and adviser after another has rejected an electoral platform based on détente, which is necessary to free funds for social progress, clamoring instead for a more anti-Soviet, pro-defense program. If a cold war manifesto by liberal Representative Stephen J. Solarz, in the *New York Times* on June 20, 1985, is any indication, that program will be a replica of Reagan's—or Reaganism with a cost-efficient face.

Nor can anything positive be said in this respect about foreign policy intellectuals with access to the media and to the Democratic Party. If such people have a useful function, it is to think unconventionally and to speak more candidly than politicians. A great many policy intellectuals are sincere cold-warriors, but many others must believe in the necessity and possibility of détente, as they said openly and often in the 1970s. Why do so few of them speak out now?

The main reason is well known but rarely publicized. Like too many congressional Democrats (and perhaps Republicans) who will not state publicly what they express privately, they are intimidated by the renewed cold war climate of political intolerance, especially on Soviet affairs.

Debate is again being stifled by censorious crusaders parading under euphemistic banners like the Committee for the Free World, Accuracy in Media and Accuracy in Academia. Once again, a galaxy of cold war publications recklessly brand anyone who dissents as being pro-Soviet, soft on Communism, a fellow traveler or an appeaser. Such intolerance has even crept into some once civil-tongued newspapers and magazines. Not long ago, a *New York Post* editorial accused ABC of "doing Yuri Andropov's job." And *The New Republic* said of a leading American expert on the Soviet Union, "With such Sovietologists, who needs the Soviets?"

And yet, given the overriding importance of U.S.-Soviet relations, it is impossible to sympathize with believers in détente who fall silent or muffle their criticism of American policy with platitudes about "bipartisan consensus," a "responsible center" and being "tough with the Soviets." Compared with the cost of political courage in other societies, the American price is cheap. Pro-détente senators who refuse to lead should step down. Policy intellectuals who prepare recipes for consumer taste should become cooks. And government officials who dissent from cold war policy only under a pseudonym, as one did in the *New York Times* in 1982, should resign.

Cold-warriors will exclaim, as they always do, "Everything is worse in the Soviet Union!" as if that should be America's standard. But no one can take pride in the fact that the nation's largest political problem is not being debated. Democratic discourse requires candor, courage and civility, and all three are woefully lacking.

[*October 12, 1985*]

A Program for Détente

VOTERS IN the 1984 Presidential election were not given a clear choice on the most fateful political issue of our time—cold war or détente with the Soviet Union. They deserve such a choice in the next election.

The nature and logical results of President Reagan's cold war policy, during his first term, were clear. American-Soviet relations were at their most dangerous stage in two decades. Most diplomatic solutions to political problems had been abandoned in favor of military ones. American troops were being readied for combat against an alleged "Soviet threat" in Central America. And a new strategic weapons race was unfolding that increased the risk of nuclear war, rendered arms control even more difficult, and made another generation of Americans captive to soaring military expenditures.

Despite those perils, the Democratic Party failed to put forward a real alternative. Indeed, its two leading candidates for the nomination seemed to have no Soviet policy at all. Both promised to end the nuclear arms race, but neither specified any diplomatic solutions to the American-Soviet *political* conflicts that underlie the arms race.

Both failed to understand, or to tell voters, the plain truth: a comprehensive policy of détente remains the only rational alternative to cold war.

What follows, therefore, is the kind of détente program that a President should advocate. It is based on three principles:

- The United States, while disliking many aspects of Soviet behavior, should recognize that the Soviet Union is a legitimate great power with equal rights and interests in world affairs. By stating this principle of political parity, the government would seek to renew and sustain a civil dialogue with the Soviet leadership and to eliminate the political reasoning behind quests for military superiority on either side.

- While seeing the Soviet Union as a powerful and dangerous adversary, the United States government should no longer exaggerate the Soviet threat to American interests or to world peace. The American people must understand that Soviet ambitions abroad are constrained by many factors other than U.S. military power and that the Soviet Union is not responsible for every incident of unrest in the world.

- The American people should have a realistic understanding of détente. It is neither appeasement nor a promise of harmonious superpower relations. Instead, it is a diplomatic process of political negotiations through which conflict between the rivals might be partially reduced by mutual accommodation and cooperation.

Having stated those principles, a pro-détente President must offer specific steps designed to begin negotiations on major American-Soviet conflicts of the last decade. Here, briefly, are a few such policies, some to be pursued publicly, others through quiet diplomacy:

1. The President announces a one-year moratorium on the testing and deployment of all American nuclear weapons and space-based antimissile systems on the condition that the Soviet leadership respond in kind. (Since the Gorbachev leadership initiated a unilateral Soviet moratorium on nuclear testing in 1985, there is every reason to think it would respond.) During that year, the two governments will reopen all arms control questions and try to improve their political relations. In addition, the President asks the Senate to demonstrate America's commitment to arms control by ratifying the 1979 SALT II treaty. He also reaffirms American adherence to the 1972 antiballistic missile treaty.

2. In order to resolve two important issues that disrupted relations in the 1970s, the President asks Congress to repeal, suspend or waive the restrictive provisions of the Jackson-Vanik and Stevenson amendments, which severely limit trade between the two countries by linking it to Jewish emigration from the Soviet Union. Disavowing economic sanctions as a policy, he pledges that only actual military technology will be excluded from trade with the Soviet Union. In return, the Soviet government must privately agree to relax existing restraints on Jewish emigration.

3. Acknowledging that both superpowers have vested political interests in the Middle East and that no lasting peace settlement there is possible without the support of both, the President asks the Soviet Union to rejoin re-

gional multilateral negotiations, from which it has been completely excluded since 1978. In return, the Soviet Union must persuade its Syrian and P.L.O. allies to recognize formally Israel's right to a secure existence. At the same time, the President also encourages the restoration of full diplomatic relations between the Soviet Union and Israel.

4. Realizing that American offers to sell weapons to Beijing have served only to provoke Soviet military anxieties and to outrage our former military ally in Taipei, the President announces a revised China policy: the United States will pursue political and economic relations with both Chinas, but it will not furnish weapons to either of them. More generally, the United States renounces the idea of any Washington-Beijing axis against the Soviet Union.

5. While deploring the Soviet war in Afghanistan, the President recalls America's difficulty in finding a way out of Vietnam. Therefore, the United States government will support any plan leading to a negotiated settlement and Soviet withdrawal.

6. The President proposes a special American-Soviet commission to draft a code of mutual restraint (including an experimental zone of military nonintervention) in the Third World, which is the scene of many indigenous wars and fruitless superpower conflicts. As the largest suppliers of arms to those regions, the United States and the Soviet Union have an obligation to replace military aid to developing countries with economic aid. To set an example, the President will consider requests for American economic assistance even from self-professed revolutionary governments providing they do not allow their countries to be

used for Soviet military bases. This policy applies to revolutionary countries in the Western Hemisphere as well, such as Cuba and Nicaragua.

Are such détente policies, and others that might reduce American-Soviet conflict in Eastern Europe and elsewhere, realistic? It is not unrealistic to think that the Soviet leadership, faced with serious cold war problems of its own at home and abroad, would respond positively to at least some of them. But because such policies would offend powerful American lobbies and constituencies, it is harder to imagine a President with the political courage to adopt them.

[*June 16, 1984, and May 1986*]

Appendix: A Short Course for General Readers

LIKE MOST Sovietologists, when public concern about American-Soviet relations is intense, I am frequently asked to recommend a book for general readers on Soviet history and politics. It is a difficult request. A great many politically motivated and ill-informed books have been written about the Soviet Union. On the other hand, knowledgeable and balanced ones often are academic in approach or style and, therefore, not easily accessible to nonspecialists.

Nor is it possible to point to a single volume that adequately covers the entire Soviet experience since 1917. If readers are willing to take on a thick textbook, I sometimes suggest Jerry F. Hough and Merle Fainsod, *How the Soviet Union Is Governed,* even though the latter chapters on contemporary politics are extremely detailed and couched in political science language. Alternately, there is my own brief scholarly book, *Rethinking the Soviet Experience: Politics and History Since 1917,* but it is considerably longer on interpretative issues than on historical and political narrative.

The best and probably only way to acquire a real understanding of the Soviet Union is to read at least one book on each of the major historical periods that shaped the system as it exists today. I offer the following course of such readings for those nonspecialists who have the necessary commitment and time. Where possible, I have chosen paperback books, which are relatively inexpensive and easily obtainable. But readers should bear in mind that my choice of titles reflects my own perspectives on the Soviet Union. There are other valuable books on each period, and many Sovietologists would recommend them over the ones I am suggesting here.

Seventy years after the Revolution, both Western scholars and Russians still debate whether Soviet Communism is a native system growing out of prerevolutionary Russian traditions or an alien import from the West. The controversy, which has large implications for foreign policy, is most interesting when argued by Russians themselves. Read together, two small books express the issues involved: on one side, the older analysis by the philosopher Nicholas Berdyaev, *The Origin of Russian Communism;* and, on the other, the more recent polemic by the writer Aleksandr Solzhenitsyn, *The Mortal Danger.*

The Russian Revolution and civil war of 1917–21 brought the Bolshevik (later Communist) Party to power and witnessed the birth of the Soviet political system. For those historic events, general readers should turn to Alexander Rabinowitch's *The Bolsheviks Come to Power* and the second volume of William Henry Chamberlin's *The Russian Revolution,* a much older but still essential book on the civil war.

Another dispute still rages, in Western scholarship and in the Soviet Union, over whether or not the extreme phenomenon of Stalinism, which arose in the early 1930s, was already predetermined by the nature of the Soviet system at the end of the civil war. It is largely a question of the political and policy alternatives present inside the Communist Party during the more liberal 1920s. That period is treated in my *Bukharin and the Bolshevik Revolution: A Political Biography, 1888–1938.* Readers who have had enough of my writings may turn to Isaac Deutscher's *The Prophet Unarmed: Trotsky, 1921–1929* or to Sheila Fitzpatrick's *The Russian Revolution,* which give different perspectives on the 1920s and the question of alternatives to Stalinism.

As for the extraordinary rule of Stalin himself, from 1929 to 1953, the biography that promises to be the richest in information and most original in interpretation is the multi-volume study by my Princeton colleague Robert C. Tucker. The first volume, *Stalin as Revolutionary,* has been published and the second, *Stalin's Revolution from Above,* will appear soon.

In addition to industrialization and collectivization, which are examined in Alec Nove's *An Economic History of the USSR,* two traumatic events under Stalin shaped the present-day Soviet system more than any other. One was Stalin's mass blood purges of the late 1930s. Here, too, readers have a choice: *The Great Terror,* by the Western scholar Robert Conquest; and *Let History Judge,* by the dissident Soviet historian Roy Medvedev. The other fateful event was, of course, the Soviet experience in World War II. Alas, there is still no full political-social history of the epic Soviet struggle against Nazi Germany, but

Harrison E. Salisbury's *The 900 Days: The Siege of Leningrad* or Alexander Werth's *Russia at War* will give readers a memorable picture of the colossal Soviet losses and heroism that led to victory.

Several books will help readers understand the leadership politics and policies of the Soviet Union since Stalin. The years of reform under Khrushchev are covered briefly and clearly in Carl A. Linden's *Khrushchev and the Soviet Leadership.* That period and Brezhnev's long reign are compared and contrasted in George Breslauer's *Khrushchev and Brezhnev as Leaders.* And the domestic and foreign problems faced by Andropov, Chernenko and Gorbachev are analyzed in *The Soviet Paradox* by Seweryn Bialer. As for the new Soviet leader, the best biography to date is Zhores A. Medvedev's *Gorbachev.*

Finally, three former American correspondents in Moscow have published books that give readers a thoughtful and gritty sense of everyday Soviet life: Hedrick Smith, *The Russians;* Robert Kaiser, *Russia;* and David K. Shipler, *Russia: Broken Idols, Solemn Dreams.* All three are valuable, but Shipler's has the special value of being the most up-to-date. Readers who want to sample a somewhat different European perspective should turn to Michael Binyon's *Life in Russia.*

Index